For a cowboy has to sing

And a cowboy has to yell,

Or his heart would break inside of him

At the gate of the home corral.

JIM BOB TINSLEY

Foreword by Roy Rogers and Dale Evans

A Collection of Sixty Romantic Cowboy and Western Songs,
Covering the Fifty-year Golden Era of Popular Standards Between 1905 and 1957

FOR A COWBOY HAS TO SING

University of Central Florida Press / Orlando

Original art done expressly for this book by
John W. Hampton, founding member of the Cowboy Artists of America.

Library of Congress
Cataloging-in-Publication Data

For a cowboy has to sing / [compiled by] Jim
Bob Tinsley : foreword by Roy Rogers and
Dale Evans.
1 score.
Cowboy songs.
ISBN 0-8130-1052-7
1. Cowboys—West (U.S.)—Songs and mu-
sic. 2. Country music—West (U.S.)
3. Popular music—West (U.S.) I. Tinsley,
Jim Bob.
M1629.6.W5F67 1991   90-48020

Half-title-page song lyrics from "A Cowboy Has To
Sing," by Bob Nolan, © 1939 Unichappell Music
Inc. and Elvis Presley Music (Renewed). All rights
on behalf of Elvis Presley Music administered by
Unichappell Music Inc. All Rights Reserved. Used
by permission.

The University of Central Florida Press is a
member of University Presses of Florida, the
scholarly publishing agency of the State Uni-
versity System of Florida. Books are selected
for publication by faculty editorial committees
at each of Florida's nine public universities:
Florida A & M University (Tallahassee), Flor-
ida Atlantic University (Boca Raton), Florida
International University (Miami), Florida State
University (Tallahassee), University of Central
Florida (Orlando), University of Florida
(Gainesville), University of North Florida
(Jacksonville), University of South Florida
(Tampa), University of West Florida
(Pensacola).

Orders for books published by all member
presses of University Presses of Florida should
be addressed to University Presses of Florida,
15 NW 15th Street, Gainesville, FL 32611.

dedicated to the dedicated: John W. Hampton

Snuff Garrett

Dottie Tinsley

Don Edwards

Michael Martin Murphey

Red Steagall

Ken Griffis

Velma Spencer

Hal Spencer

Clara "P-Nuts" Nolan

Hi Busse

Guy Logsdon

Justine McCoy

Billy Joe Rogers

Ormly Gumfudgin

members of the Western Music Association

Jim Steinblatt, ASCAP

Andy Erish, American Vaudeville, Inc.

Hermon Rahn (who taught

"South of the Border"

to an Italian prisoner he

captured in World War II)

and

the memory of Bob Dunn and Zeb Robinson

who "ride on the other shore"

CONTENTS

Happy Trails
Roy Rogers
to
Dale Evans

FOREWORD

Roy Rogers & Dale Evans

In *For A Cowboy Has to Sing*, Jim Bob Tinsley has rounded up and cut out sixty prime specimens of popular cowboy and western music. Finally we have a book that tells us the who, where, when, why, and how of popular cowboy songs.

Like a welcoming campfire on a cold night, the title alone sparks warm memories for the two of us. It comes from a song written by an old friend of Roy's, Bob Nolan, who along with Tim Spencer and Roy started up a singing group called the Pioneers Trio in 1933. Later, as the Sons of the Pioneers, they recorded more than half the songs in this collection and sang nearly all the rest at rodeos and shows.

Reading the histories Jim Bob has gathered on each of the songs is like saddling up a good cow horse and riding back along the western music trail. Remember the old radio shows—"Hollywood Barn Dance," "Log Cabin Dude Ranch," Gene Autry's "Melody Ranch"? How about Bob Wills and His Texas Playboys, or Laura Lee Owens, the Queen of Western Swing? And those wonderful western movies—*Cimarron, The Trail of the Lonesome Pine, Rhythm on the Range* with Bing Crosby, and *Under Western Stars*—would have all been G-rated (if there'd been a rating system then), and they still would have been big hits.

Some of these sagebrush serenades carry a lot of personal meaning for the two of us. As Jim Bob records, Dale wrote "Happy Trails" forty years ago and it became Roy's theme song. In the Westerns he made for Republic Pictures, Roy strummed and sang enough of these songs to load down a couple of lop-eared pack mules. He serenaded Trigger with "Ole Faithful" in *My Pal Trigger*, and he sang "I'm an Old Cowhand," by Johnny Mercer (who couldn't read music), in *King of the Cowboys*. In *Hollywood Canteen* he sang "Don't Fence Me In," by Montana songwriter and poet Bob Fletcher (not entirely by Cole Porter, as Jim Bob reminds us many people believed). And he sang "When It's Night-time in Nevada," by Richard Pascoe, H. O'Reilly Clint, and Will Dulmage, in the movie of the same name, and "The Utah Trail," by Bob Palmer, in *Utah*, which starred both of us along with Gabby Hayes.

Along with the trip down Western music's memory lane, Jim Bob has rustled up a whole corral full of little-known facts about these songs that will keep readers as fascinated and entertained as tenderfeet at their first roundup. Just to get your curiosity up: The man who wrote "Mexicali Rose" ran for vice president of the United States on a ticket with General Douglas MacArthur. A high school student in Utah wrote the lyrics to "When It's Springtime in the Rockies." "Tumbling Tumbleweeds" started out as "tumblin' leaves" (that's the Sons of the Pioneers' theme song, by the way, and Bob Nolan wrote that, too, along with another great cowboy song in this book, "Cool Water"). "The Hills of Old Wyomin'" was written for the movie *Palm Springs* by two songwriters who never had been to Wyoming.

Another wonderful thing about this book is that

it gives credit to many songwriters who for years have gone unknown and unrecognized for their great contributions to cowboy and western music. So often we remember who recorded a song instead of who wrote it. And even though some of the writers of these songs actually were ranch hands and wranglers, readers might be surprised at how many were professional musicians and at how many of these songs got written in the shadows of sky-scrapers instead of mountains, accompanied by the sounds of city traffic instead of the lonely howl of a coyote.

Sitting down with *For A Cowboy Has to Sing* has reminded the two of us how blessed we were to be a part of the glory days of western movies in Hollywood, the 1930s, 1940s, and 1950s, when the singing cowboy left his brand on popular music. Those were the days when the good guys wore white hats and always won, and the toughest choice facing most little buckaroos was whether to buy popcorn or Raisinets. With this collection, a highly respected country and western music historian has brought us a whole new level of appreciation for those days when our heroes and heroines rode tall in the saddle and life seemed simple and clear as a prairie night under the stars.

Happy trails,

Roy Rogers

Dale Evans

INTRODUCTION

The early songs written about the cowboy and the western scene differ from the ones that originated among the cowboys themselves. What recorded-music historian Ulysses "Jim" Walsh calls "cow-punch compositions"* were written as marketable products, published and copyrighted by a bevy of talented writers with diverse backgrounds, some of whom may never have been west of eastern suburbs or may not have even known which end of a cow the hay went in. A number of bona fide cowboys did write and publish commercially successful songs a few years later, but the earliest published songs about the colorful herdsman came from the imagination of Tin Pan Alley writers in New York City, who had commercial incentives when they hit the trail of western songwriting. Even jazz innovators George and Ira Gershwin, most often associated with symphonic orchestrations, fell under the spell of sagebrush.

The great era of popular cowboy compositions and closely allied romantic western songs spanned the first half of the twentieth century. Max S. Witt, German-born songwriter with the Joseph W. Stern Company in New York, wrote a cowboy love song, "My Heart's To-night in Texas 'By the Silvery Rio Grande,'" in 1900, with lyrics by poet-author Robert F. Roden. Without the benefit of record sales and extensive promotion, the song failed to attain nationwide popularity but did enter the public domain. In the 1920s it reappeared in various collections of cowboy songs that listed the song's origins as unknown.

The pace-setting "Cheyenne" gave the first impetus to popular cowboy songs. A 1905 love song with a basic "wooed and won" theme, it included what may be the only tuneful "You will or you'll walk home!" ultimatum to a reluctant female.

An eager audience was assured during this period. Dime novels out of New York with adventure stories about the daring saddlemen of the cattle country already had captivated American readers. Cowboys had appeared as incidental characters in paperbound stories in the 1870s, but the first time one became a central figure in a novel was in an 1882 Beadle's Dime Library edition entitled *Parson Jim, King of the Cowboys; or, The Gentle Shepherd's Big "Clean Out,"* by Frederick Whittaker. The leading character was a Harvard divinity student suffering from consumption, who went west to regain his health and ended up in Muleville, Colorado. In one year his health had been restored, he had learned the skills of the cowboy, and ultimately he was elected to the state assembly as a champion of the downtrodden.*

It was largely through the efforts of the great promoter himself, William F. "Buffalo Bill" Cody, that the cowboy gained international fame as the foremost symbol of the American West. "The Wild West," sometimes called "Hon. W. F. Cody and Dr. W. F. Carver's Rocky Mountain and Prairie

*Jim Walsh, "'Cowboy Song' Recordings," *Hobbies* 81, no. 4, pt. 3 (June 1976): 36.

*Daryl Jones, *The Dime Novel Western* (Bowling Green, Ohio: Bowling Green University Popular Press, 1978), 99–102.

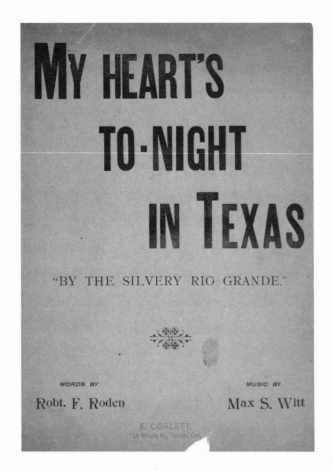

Cowboy movie star Ken Maynard singing to his co-star Edith Roberts in the 1929 Universal Maynard production *The Wagon Master*. (Saturday Matinee)

Exposition," opened for the first time in May 1883, in Omaha, Nebraska. One of the featured acts was William Levi "Buck" Taylor, billed as the "King of the Cowboys." He became America's first cowboy hero in fact as well as in fiction.

Taylor was a true cowboy, born in Fredericksburg, Texas, in 1857. Nineteen years later he helped drive 1,500 cattle north to Ogallala, Nebraska, where the entire herd was sold to Cody and a ranching partner, Major Frank North. The cowboy was then hired as a ranch hand by the buyers and later became a star performer in the Wild West

Bentley Ball, pioneer recorder of cowboy songs. (*Columbia Catalog*, 1919 Supplement)

extravaganzas of the famed Indian fighter and master showman.

Prentiss Ingraham, press agent for Buffalo Bill, wrote the first "cheap fiction" involving a cowboy hero for Beadle's now Half-Dime Library in 1887. It was entitled *Buck Taylor, King of the Cowboys; or, The Raiders and the Rangers*. By the end of 1891, Ingraham had written six more tales about the newly discovered hero. As with all dime novelists, Ingraham downplayed the hardships and drudgery of the life of the true cowboy in favor of a thrilling and carefree fictional life that centered around his dispensation of social justice.

One of the earliest and most popular of all fictional cowboys was Young Wild West, portrayed for twenty-five years in the *Wild West Weekly* of Frank Tousey. Between 1902 and 1927 a grand total of 1,296 issues of the magazine featured the cowboy idol of so-called subliterature, who was found as an infant by a cavalry group at the scene of an Indian attack. The commander of the detachment bestowed his own surname, West, upon the orphan. Troopers called the baby boy "Young" for obvious reasons, and to suit the time and place they added the middle name "Wild," the name the future hero preferred.*

*J. Edward Leithead, "Young Wild West," *Dime Novel Round-Up* 19, no. 7 (July 1951): 49.

Above: The dime novel Buck Taylor, c. 1905. (Courtesy Buffalo Bill Historical Center, Cody, Wyoming)

Below: The real life Buck Taylor, c. 1900. (Courtesy Buffalo Bill Historical Center, Cody, Wyoming)

Cowboy enthusiasts had also been enchanted by eastern authors like Bret Harte, the New Yorker who went west to write. But it was with the appearance in 1902 of the first great American cowboy novel, *The Virginian: A Horseman of the Plains*, that a cowboy hero captured all America. Written by Harvard-educated Owen Wister, who also followed trails west for inspiration, this cowboy classic was reprinted fifteen times during its first year of publication.

In addition, *The Great Train Robbery* was filmed by the Edison Company in 1903, on location in New Jersey. It is generally considered the first western motion picture, although five years earlier the same company had shot a brief tableau called *Cripple Creek Bar-room* in which a number of cowboy dandies were featured.

So, from the outset of popular cowboy love songs in 1905, cylinder phonographs began grinding away musical releases about the newly adopted American hero. By 1912 the cylinder gave way to single- and double-faced discs, but the cowboy vogue continued riding high western style.

For more than a decade, cowboy songs originating in the East were performed in vaudeville sketches and in music halls by show troupes of professionally trained singers accompanied by full orchestras. Vocal soloists Billy Murray, Len Spencer, and "The Singing Policeman," Eddie Morton, gained considerable fame for their renditions of popular cowboy songs on phonograph records. Numerous male quartets, including the original Christy Minstrels, also recorded the songs for a ready market.

Some overlapping of traditional and composed cowboy songs occurred during the transition from scattered range audiences of cows to jammed houses of music hall patrons on Broadway. A few published songs by westerners like Curley Fletcher, Carson J. Robison, Tex Owens, and Gene Autry became part of the cowboy genre. Often passing along these songs orally without knowing who wrote them, successive singers did not always realize that they had helped these songs attain a traditional status not achieved by others.

The first commercial recording of "handed-down" cowboy songs was issued in September 1919 on a double-faced Columbia disc that introduced "Jesse James" and "The Dying Cowboy." The two renditions by Bentley Ball, a Virginia student of American folk songs and a singer at popular "Song-a-Logues" (a forerunner of modern sing-a-longs) throughout the country, were presented more in the manner of a concert artist than in a rough-and-ready folksy style.

The western song scenario began to expand in all directions in the 1920s with the subjects of new compositions ranging from lighthearted love to a quest for a home in the West, and from nostalgia for the Rockies in the springtime to a longing to be in Texas when the sage was blooming. All indicate a strong desire to get away from Broadway and other eastern city lights. Singing performers Vernon Dalhart, Carl Sprague, and Jules Verne Allen, all with cow country backgrounds in Texas, began to record authentic cowboy songs during the same decade.

Parts of "I'd Like to Be in Texas When They Round Up in the Spring" may be traditional, but in 1925 the song was sung and printed sheet music copies were hawked at a convention of Texas cattlemen in Fort Worth. Two years later it was copyrighted by the same singing promoter who attributed its writing to a couple of fellow Texans.

A number of eastern composers moved to California in the late 1920s and early 1930s and began writing songs and musical scores for western movies in Hollywood. Their efforts then took on added sophistication and reflected a better knowledge of the subject. Even with expanding radio programming and recordings by big bands and influential singing stars like Bing Crosby and Rudy Vallee, the nationwide introduction of cowboy songs through movie westerns, more than through any other medium, probably accounts for their prodigious growth in popularity during the thirties.

On 6 October 1929, Ken Maynard became the first singing cowboy movie star with the release of the part-talking film *The Wagon Master*, a Universal Maynard Production, in which he sang "The Lone Star Trail" and "The Cowboy's Lament." Although the motion picture was 40 percent silent footage, it offered the Texas-born cowboy his first talking role. *Variety* called the transitional film, co-starring Edith Roberts, "a pioneer in the field of dialog and sound effects for small-time westerns."[*]

Just about every popular singer, concert artist, and orchestra of the day gave widespread exposure in 1933 to "Home on the Range," a little-known folk song of the West. Live radio broadcasts daily on all principal networks gave it a popularity never before attained by an American song. Ballad collector John Lomax had discovered the song through oral transmission in San Antonio in 1908, and more than three decades later he labeled it "the folksong national anthem."[†]

Also in 1933, Billy Hill's immortal composition "The Last Round-Up" hit the radio air waves. With the help of pulp westerns, Zane Grey novels, radio broadcasts, sound movies, and the unprecedented outpouring of new cowboy songs during the next ten years, all America was singing, humming, or enjoying cowboy and western songs.

Trail songs of popular composers, unlike traditional ballads, represent the "Happy Trails" image promoted by Roy Rogers and Dale Evans, with no hint of cattle, stampedes, or violent death. Rarely considered major cattle outlets, the Utah Trail, the Navajo Trail, and the Santa Fe Trail of song were merely musical settings for splendor and romance.

The writing of sentimental cowboy songs began to decline with the rise of so-called adult westerns. The fifty-year golden era of popular standards faded soon after the appearance of the 1952 Academy Award classic, "High Noon." This distinctively new type of cowtown song delved into the inner feelings of a newlywed lawman who was deserted by townspeople and compelled by conscience and duty to face a quartet of desperate gunmen alone in a street shootout, or else lie a

[*]"Film Reviews," *Variety* 94, no. 12 (2 October 1929): 22.
[†]John A. Lomax, "Half-Million Dollar Song—Origin of 'Home on the Range,'" *Southwest Review* 31, no. 1 (Fall 1945): 1.

coward in his grave. Another romantic tragedy, the lengthy musical saga "El Paso" written in 1957 by Arizona-born Marty Robbins, seems to have ended the glorious heyday of musical adoration for the man on horseback. The gamut had run from the almost flippant idealism of carefree lovers on broncos to the stark realism of border romance between a cowboy and a cantina hustler that ended in death by the gun.

1 Cheyenne
1905

The appearance of "Hiawatha" in 1903 set the pace for pseudo-Indian songs, followed a year later by "Navajo," the top Indian hit of 1904. Two youthful Tin Pan Alley composers, Egbert Van Alstyne and Harry Williams, based the latter song on a humorous theme of a black man proposing to a Navajo girl and promising to supply feathers for her hair if chickens were near. The clever musical satire "Napanee" of 1906 tells of a disillusioned "paleface" whose Indian wife keeps presenting him with papooses in numbers while she grows older and jaded. A more serious love song of a warrior bold and his lovely little "Red Wing,"

probably the most enduring of all Indian song compositions, appeared in 1907.

In the midst of this brief heyday of Indian songs appeared the first successful commercial song about the American cowboy. Capitalizing on the apparent interest of musical audiences in western romance, Van Alstyne and Williams combined their talents in 1905 to produce "Cheyenne," celebrating the romantic cowboy for the first time in an American hit song.

Van Alstyne and Williams were both midwesterners. Egbert Anson Van Alstyne was born in Marengo, Illinois, on 5 March 1878. At the age of

Williams and Van Alstyne
(From the sheet music cover of
"Oh That Navajo Rag,"
Jerome H. Remick & Co.,
New York and Detroit, 1911)

1

seven, he played the organ in the Methodist Sunday school he attended. Later he toured the West as a pianist for various stage shows, but he went broke in Nogales, Mexico.

On the road again as a song plugger, Van Alstyne met Harry Hiram Williams of Faribault, Minnesota, who was born on 23 August 1879, and was to become his songwriting partner. The two toured with a circus and appeared in vaudeville acts until 1900, when they moved to New York and began writing songs while living on the salary Van Alstyne made as a staff pianist for music publisher Jerome H. Remick. In 1905 they produced "In the Shade of the Old Apple Tree," one of America's greatest song hits.

Believing that a song about a cowboy's love affair would make them money, Van Alstyne and Williams wrote "Cheyenne" later that year, punning the title with the name and disposition of the cowgirl subject, "Shy Ann." Famed recording artist Billy Murray, known as "The Denver Nightingale," recorded the song, complete with cowboy "yips" and the sound of a trotting horse, for the Victor Talking Machine Company in July 1906. A printed supplement promoting the recording described the single-faced disc:

> A jolly "cowboy" song telling of the wild ride of a cowboy and his sweetheart to Cheyenne, sixty-seven miles away, in search of a preacher to marry them. At the threshold "Shy Ann" has a fit of shyness and proposes to go back. "If you do you walk," says Mr. Cowboy, and at the thought of a sixty-seven mile tramp the lady blushingly consents. Splendidly sung by Murray, with descriptive effects by the orchestra.*

Using the same rhyming combination of maiden and town, early country music entertainer Dwight Butcher wrote "Shy Little Anne from Cheyenne" in 1940.

Identical in title to the 1905 "Cheyenne" is the title song for the popular Warner Brothers television series "Cheyenne," written exactly fifty years later by Stan Jones and William Lava. Clint Walker played the title role of Cheyenne, a cowboy loner who drifted from place to place—as the song says—like reckless clouds.

---

*Jim Walsh, "'Cowboy Song' Recordings," *Hobbies* 81, no. 2, pt. 1 (April 1976): 130.

Cheyenne.

(Shy Ann.)

Words by HARRY WILLIAMS.　　　　　　　　Music by EGBERT VAN ALSTYNE.

Allegro moderato.

Way out in old Wy – o – ming long a – go, ___
They rode that night and near – ly half the day, ___

Where coy – otes lurk while night winds howl and blow, ___ A
Chey – enne was six – ty sev – en miles a – way, ___ But

cow – boys lus – ty voice rang out "Hel – lo!" _____ And
when at last they gal – loped up the street, _____ The

ech – oed thro' the val – ley down be – low, _____
cow – boy's pride was real – ly hard to beat, _____

Then came back a maid – en's an – swer sweet and clear, _____
On his arm his fu – ture bride a – car – ry – ing, _____

Cow – boy tossed his hat up in the air, _____ Said
But be – neath the lit – tle church – es dome, _____ Said

he "I've come to take you right a-way from here,_____ Chey-
she "I feel like turn-ing back, not mar-ry-ing,"_____ His

enne, they say, is miles a-way but they've a preach-er there," Then
face got red, and then he said, "You will or you'll walk home, If

she just drooped her eye, She was so ver-y shy, So
you ride back to - day, You'll hon-or and o-bey," I

poco a poco rit.

shy, oh, my, and then he made re - ply, Oh! Oh! Oh!
do, I do, then he was heard to say, Oh! Oh! Oh!

a tempo

2 San Antonio 1907

"San Antonio," the second cowboy song hit by the songwriting team of Egbert Van Alstyne and Harry Williams, appeared early in 1907. An advertisement placed in *Variety* on 30 March by Jerome H. Remick & Company called it "absolutely the greatest of all cowboy songs. A hit the world over."*

The new song had a complete turnabout in plot from that of its predecessor, "Cheyenne," in which Shy Ann hopped upon her lover's pony with him and rode off to town to get married. By comparison, the more capricious girlfriend in "San Antonio" hopped upon her lover's pony without him and rode away with a "tenderfoot." The rejected suitor, surprisingly forgiving, revealed to his partner that he was willing to take her back if she was not happy with her new fascination.

In April 1907, the Rambler Minstrel Company, of which Billy Murray was a member, recorded "San Antonio" on Zon-o-phone and Columbia records. Edison issued the song by Billy Murray and a chorus the following month. Victor issued a version during the same month by Billy Murray and the Christy Minstrels.

Two years later, Van Alstyne and Williams wrote the light-hearted Broadway-cowboy song "He Was a Cowboy," which was sung by Dave Montgomery and Fred Stone in the Charles Dillingham stage production *The Old Town*. The musical began a run of 171 performances on 10 January 1909, in the

brand-new Globe Theatre in New York City. In the lyrics to the new song was a plug for the hit song "Navajo," composed in 1903 by the same twosome:

He was a cowboy, a cowboy in a show;
He rode a bucking broncho while the band
    played "Navajo." "YIP!"
He was a cowboy who met his Waterloo;
He thought he was a badman 'till he struck
    Eighth Avenue.

Harry Williams went to Hollywood in 1915. His screen career as an actor and director of silent film comedies included two years with film producer and director Mack Sennett; one year with comic actor, director, and script writer Roscoe "Fatty" Arbuckle; six months with Fox Sunshine Comedies; and one year with Toyo Film Company of Japan. Part of his film work was on the popular "Snookie" comedies.

During a songwriting alliance with Charles N. Daniels, better known as Neil Morét, Williams wrote "Mickey," the first movie theme song written to exploit a motion picture. The recurrent melody ran throughout the background score in the classic 1918 silent western by the same name. The film was produced by Mack Sennett and released by Paramount. The gifted Keystone comedienne Mabel Normand played the title role in which she displayed her "wild and woolly West" bareback riding ability.

A month before his death Williams was in New

Variety 6, no. 3 (30 March 1907): 20.

Egbert Van Alstyne (ASCAP)

Harry H. Williams (Academy
of Motion Picture Arts and
Sciences)

York to place his latest composition, "Bobolink," with Jerome H. Remick & Company. On the return trip to the West Coast he was stricken with a complication of bronchitis-influenza, and he died on 15 May 1922 at his mother's home in Oakland, California.

Egbert Van Alstyne spent his songwriting career in New York and Chicago, rejecting all offers from Hollywood. In addition to a continuous output of hit songs, he wrote the scores for eight Broadway musicals during the first decade of the century. His "Good-a-bye, John" was the only number ever interpolated into a Victor Herbert score. Van Alstyne was a staff member with Jerome H. Remick & Company for forty years; during that time he had more than five hundred of his own songs listed in their catalogs.

"This Is My Song," composed in 1938 with lyrics by Gus Kahn, was Van Alstyne's last published song with Jerome H. Remick & Company. He died in Chicago on 9 July 1951 at the age of seventy-three.

SAN ANTONIO

Words by
HARRY WILLIAMS

Music by
EGBERT VAN ALSTYNE

Bill says "Come down Pal, Down in - to town Pal, Big time for me and
I wont re - sent it I might have spent it Plung-ing with Fa - ro

you,＿＿＿＿ Don't mind your old gal you know its "Cold" Pal,
Jack＿＿＿＿ If she's not hap - py there with her chap - pie

If what you say is true＿＿＿＿ "Where is she now" Bill
Tell her I'll take her back＿＿＿＿ No ten-der foot like

cried＿＿＿＿ And his part - ner just re - plied＿＿＿＿
him＿＿＿＿ Could love her like her boy Jim＿＿＿＿

CHORUS.

San An - to - ni   An - to - ni - o   She hopped up

on a po - ny and ran a - way with To - ny If you

see her just let me know   and I'll meet you   in

San An-to-ni - o.   -o.

3 Pride of the Prairie 1907

Taking advantage of the new public fancy for cowboy songs, the enterprising duo of George Botsford and Henry J. Breen wrote "Pride of the Prairie" in 1907. Like the vogue-setting "Cheyenne," the theme of the new song was a shy girl's consent to marry a cowboy and to ride away with him on his bronco across the plains to have the ceremony performed.

When a Columbia recording by the Peerless Quartet was released the following year, the song was described as "the best song of the Western plains that has been produced. It is full of the fine, broad swing of 'cowboy' music, which is rapidly becoming the leading feature of the big musical successes.*

"Pride of the Prairie" has the distinction of being the first American cowboy song to become a hit in the British Isles, where it was recorded more extensively and remained popular longer than in the United States. The haunting melody was written by George Botsford, who later became one of the truly great American ragtime composers.

Botsford and Breen combined talents again in 1908 to write "Denver Town":

Tell your Pony that your Heart is lonely,
He'll take you flying into Denver Town.

George C. Botsford was born on 24 February 1874, in Sioux Falls, Dakota Territory, and his

*Jim Walsh, "'Cowboy Song' Recordings," *Hobbies* 81, no. 6, pt. 5 (August 1976): 53.

family moved to Iowa when George was eleven. His professional life, however, was spent as a composer-conductor in New York City. In addition to his songwriting, Botsford was a musical director for vaudeville productions and arranged music for minstrel shows. He also wrote arrangements for popular male quartets and quintets that had been hired by early recording companies in New York.

Harry Breen, the "poet laureate of vaudeville." (*National Vaudeville Artists Eighth Annual Benefit*, 1924)

American ragtime composer
George Botsford. (*The Metro-nome*, September 1923)

their songs became as popular as "Pride of the Prairie." Breen wrote special songs and materials for female vaudeville monologues and was noted for his extemporaneous rhyming on stage. Following two published volumes of poems on his memories, reflections, and eulogies, he became known as "the poet laureate of vaudeville."

Harry Breen collapsed on stage at Loew's Capitol Theatre in Atlanta, Georgia, on 9 February 1929, and died two days later of heart failure. In a book of his poetry, *Loon Lyrics and Others*, Breen had already made a burial request:

When I book the final day,
And I'm dead I want to lay
With my head turned towards the Battery
And my feet towards old Broadway.*

* Harry Breen, *Loon Lyrics and Others* (Boston: Gardner & Taplin Co., 1913), 46–47.

Botsford's second ragtime song, "Black and White Rag," written in 1908, established him as a professional songwriter. His "Grizzly Bear Rag," written in 1910, to which Irving Berlin later added lyrics, helped launch a new dance craze by the same name in which both partners clasped each other in a bear hug and rocked from side to side in time with the beat.

Following his initial songwriting successes, Botsford was hired by Jerome H. Remick & Company as an arranger and head of the harmony and quartet departments. He died in New York City on 1 February 1949.

Two names of lyricists appear on the sheet music to "Pride of the Prairie." On the inside it is Henry J. Breen; on the front cover it is Harry Breen. They were one and the same. Henry J. Breen became a renowned vaudeville comic monologist and musical parodist as Harry Breen, but for an assured identity with his most famous song he used both bylines.

Breen was born on the Lower East Side of New York City in 1878. He began his career as a song plugger for Shapiro, Bernstein & Company. Keith agent Ed S. Keller saw him perform at Coney Island in 1904 and booked the act for vaudeville. Breen wrote a number of songs in his spare time with another collaborator, Tom Geary, but none of

Pride Of The Prairie

Words by
HENRY J. BREEN.

Music by
GEORGE BOTSFORD.

1. Out in the wild and wooly Prai - rie Not far from old Pu- eb-lo
2. When o'er the prai-rie day was break ing And all was qui-et on the

town _____ There lived a lit-tle girl named Ma - ry,
plains _____ Then to his Ma-ry he was say - ing

CHORUS.

Pride of the prai - rie, Ma - ry my own,

Jump up be - side me, ride to my home,

My heart's been las - soed, No more we'll roam, Pride of the

Prai - rie Ma - ry!_____   Ma - ry!_____

Ma - ry Ma - ry quite contra - ry.

4 My Pony Boy
1909

"**M**y Pony Boy," generally referred to simply as "Pony Boy," is one of the great popular songs of all time and is probably better remembered than any other early romantic cowboy song.

The Columbia Quartet recorded "My Pony Boy" in September 1909, on a Columbia label. The following month an Edison recording on an Amberol cylinder was released featuring singer Ada Jones and a male quartet. Along with a male chorus, the same Miss Jones recorded the song in November for Victor. The Peerless Quartet also recorded it for Victor in 1909. These and subsequent recordings gave the song immense popularity throughout America.

The Melody Monarchs were a vaudeville act that featured four male pianists at four pianos on stage. Two members of the group, Bobby Heath and Charley O'Donnell, collaborated in 1909 to write "My Pony Boy." Both were Philadelphians. Born a year apart, they died a year and an ocean apart both at age sixty-three.

Bobby Heath was the professional name of Robin Frear, chosen partly because he wanted to perpetuate a surname in his immediate ancestry. He was born into an old theatrical family on 1 December 1889, and started in show business at the age of eight. Four years later he was appearing in Frank Dumont's Minstrels in Philadelphia as a blackface boy comic who sang and danced. Heath spent many years in vaudeville and later produced his own tabloid revues. He wrote the words to "My Pony Boy."

Charles O'Donnell was born in 1888. His songwriting fame in America is based primarily on his composition of the music to "My Pony Boy."

"My Pony Boy" and "Shine on Harvest Moon" were introduced in 1909 as additional songs in the Broadway production *Miss Innocence* starring Anna Held, saucy French singer and wife of Florenz Ziegfeld. Both songs were performed by Lillian Lorraine. The musical revue was in its second year, having opened in November of the previous year.

Heath and O'Donnell teamed up again in 1910 with another romantic cowboy song simply entitled "Cowboy." This effort did not achieve the popularity of its predecessor. It tells of the successful entreaties to a cowboy by a girl with matrimony on her mind.

> Cowboy, come kiss me now, boy,
>   Please show me how, boy,
> To love you, yes, you'd make an awful hit,
>   If you would spoon a little bit,
> So please me, but don't you tease me,
>   And we will ride, we will glide
> O'er the mountains, My cowboy!

Bobby Heath later played the Keith circuit with his own troupe and wrote such song hits as "On the Old Back Porch," "In the Sweet Long Ago," "All the Pretty Girls in Town," "Just a Quaker Town," "Roll 'Em Girls Roll 'Em," and "When Mr. Cupid Comes to Town." Before his retirement, "Pony Boy" Heath was an entertainer and master of ceremonies in the popular New York nightclub Sawdust Trail. He died in Philadelphia on 4 March 1952.

Around 1911 Charles O'Donnell moved to England, where he introduced Dixieland music. With Eddie Fields he formed The Two Rascals, singing ragtime songs at the old Alhambra Palace Music Hall at Leicester Square in London. Later their act became The Three Rascals with personnel changing from time to time. For a while the group disbanded, but it reappeared during World War II as The Two Rascals & Jacobson, consisting once again of O'Donnell and Fields with pianist Jess Jacobson.

Under the glittering lights of London's West End where he was once a star, Charles "Dixieland" O'Donnell collapsed and died from poison on the night of 17 September 1951. Although wealthy at one time, he was penniless when he died.

A copy of "My Pony Boy" was buried in the time capsule at the New York World Fair in 1940 as a representive of contemporary American life.

My Pony Boy

Words by
BOBBY HEATH

Music by
CHARLEY O'DONNELL

1. Way out west, in a nest from the rest, dwelt the best-est lit-tle
2. Till one day, out that way, so they say, came to stay a Fluf-fy-

Bron-cho-Boy;_____ He could ride, he could glide o'er the
Ruf-fle girl._____ She made eyes, she sur-prised, and he

prai - ries like an ar - row._____ Ev' - ry
found his heart was las - soed._____ When he

maid in the glade, was a - fraid he would trade his lit - tle
thought he was caught, how he fought, but she taught this po - ny -

heart a - way,_____ So each lit - tle peach made a
boy to love._____ But he balked when she talked of a

nice lit - tle speech of love to him.
trip to New York, so she sang to him:_

REFRAIN

Po - ny Boy, Po - ny Boy, Won't you be my To - ny Boy?

Don't say no. Here we go Off a - cross the plains; Mar-ry me,

Car - ry me Right a - way with you__ Gid - dy up, gid-dy up,

gid-dy up, *Whoa!* My Po - ny Boy

Boy

My Pony Boy

Quartet for Male or Mixed Voices

REFRAIN: *(Melody in 2nd Tenor or Soprano.)*

arr. by RIBÉ DANMARK

5
Ragtime Cow Boy Joe
1912

In the mid-1890s, the term *ragtime* was applied to a uniquely American variety of musical expression. This innovative rhythmic pattern, called syncopation, features a conflicting beat superimposed between regular accents. It is basically Afro-American music that evolved through cultural exchange and is the first defined ingredient of jazz, said by some to be the only popular music indigenous to America.

Many old-time rags had little merit beyond rhythmic energy. "Ragtime Cow Boy Joe," however, is unusual in its clever combination of rhythm and rhyme. The amusing toe-tapping number was created in 1912 by a trio of early Tin Pan Alley writers—Grant Clarke, Lewis F. Muir, and Maurice Abrahams. The original Ragtime Cow Boy Joe was four-year-old Joseph Abrahams, a nephew of Maurice Abrahams. The child liked to dress up in a cowboy suit, complete with boots and wide-brimmed hat, and his uncle introduced him to fellow songwriters as "little ragtime-cowboy Joe" whenever they dropped by for a visit.

Grant Clarke decided to be a songwriter in New York after trouping around the country as an actor for a few years. "Young man, you're wasting your time. You'll never be a songwriter," a music publisher told him after looking over his first efforts.

With young Joseph Abrahams in mind, Clarke sat up that same night and wrote song lyrics about an adult ragtime-cowboy Joe. The next morning he prevailed upon his friends Lewis F. Muir and Maurice Abrahams to write a melody for the words.

Muir took the completed song to the same publisher who had turned Clarke down. To conceal his identity, Clarke stayed in a barroom across the street and waited for a signal from Muir that the song had been accepted. It was not long in coming. Their outwitting of the publisher was a big joke around Tin Pan Alley for years.*

Grant C. Clarke was born on 14 May 1891, in Akron, Ohio. He became one of Broadway's pioneer songwriters. Associated with publisher Leo Feist as well as Shapiro, Bernstein & Company, Clarke later formed a partnership in the music publishing business with Edgar Leslie. His "Second Hand Rose," written with composer James Hanley, was sung in the *Ziegfeld Follies of 1921*.

When motion pictures began using theme songs, Clarke was already in Hollywood. His first one was "Mother, I Still Have You," which Al Jolson sang in *The Jazz Singer* in 1927.

While singing "I'm the Medicine Man For Your Blues," a song he had written for bandleader Ted Lewis, Clarke collapsed and died from acute alcholism at a drinking party in Hollywood on 16 May 1931. He had written more than two hundred copyrighted songs, with fifty-eight hits to his credit.

In 1912, the same year Lewis F. Muir wrote the music to "Ragtime Cow Boy Joe" with help from fellow composer Maurice Abrahams, he also

---

*Damon Runyon [probable author], "Grant Clarke," typescript, 5 pp., n.d., in Clarke memorabilia owned by Carl W. Magnuson, San Diego, California.

Maurice Abrahams (Depart-
ment of Special Collections,
UCLA)

Grant Clarke (Courtesy of Carl
W. Magnuson)

Lewis F. Muir (*Current Opinion*, December 1915)

wrote the time-honored favorite "Waiting For the
Robert E. Lee."

Muir was born Louis Frank Meuer in New York
City on 30 May 1883. He was a tramp for five years
before becoming a millinery peddler in the West.
He went from selling hats to playing the piano in
Chicago cafés and honky-tonks in St. Louis. Muir
died at thirty-two in New York City on 3 December 1915.

Maurice Abrahams (Maurie Abrams) was born in
Russia on 18 March 1883, and came to America
when he was two years old. He spent most of his
life in New York City, where he was a music publisher for twenty-five years and wrote special material for his wife, Belle Baker, the vaudeville star.
He died at forty-eight on 13 April 1931.

"Ragtime Cow Boy Joe" was revived in 1943 by
Alice Faye in the Twentieth Century motion pic-
ture *Hello, Frisco, Hello*. Two years later Betty
Hutton sang the song in *Incendiary Blonde*, a
Paramount picture based on the life of Miss Texas
Guinan, who had entered silent motion pictures in
1917 as a "hellbent-for-leather" cowgirl in two-reel
Western films. During the wild Prohibition days of
bootleg gin, whiskey, and applejack, Texas
Guinan was the hostess and operator of garish
speakeasies in New York City and on the West
Coast. A steady patron of the establishment in
California was Grant Clarke.

"Ragtime Cow Boy Joe."

Words by
GRANT CLARKE.

Music by
LEWIS F. MUIR.
MAURICE ABRAHAMS.

man by far,___ Is Rag - time Cow Boy Joe. _____
town is Joe's, ___ 'Cause he's a rag - time bear. ___

fz

Got his name from sing - ing to the cows and sheep__
When he starts a spiel - ing on the dance hall floor__

Ev - ry night they say he sings the herd to sleep
No one but a lu - na - tic would start a war,

In a bass - o rich and deep_ Croon - ing soft and low. ___
Wise men know_ his for - ty four_ Makes men dance for fair. ___

hear that fel - low's gun Be - cause the West - ern folks all

know, He's a high - fa - lut - ing scoot - ing, shoot - ing

son - of - a - gun from Ar - iz - o - na, Rag time Cow Boy

Joe._____ He al - ways Joe._____

fz

D. S.

6

I'd Like to Be in Texas When
They Round Up in the Spring 1916

William Alonzo Fishback, singer and first publisher of "I'd Like to Be in Texas When They Round Up in the Spring," was born on 26 December 1886 in Fort Worth. He successfully introduced the song in 1925 under the name Lon Fishback, "The Singing Cowboy," and copyrighted it two years later, giving credit for writing the song to fellow Texans Jack C. Williams and Carl Copeland.

Lon Fishback was a member of the radio Chuck Wagon Gang, sponsored in the 1930s by the Bewley Mills Flour Company. The group followed the noontime show of the equally popular Light Crust Doughboys on the weekly statewide Texas Quality Network.

Jack C. Williams of Fort Worth had an unpublished copy of "I'd Like to Be in Texas When They Round Up in the Spring" copyrighted on 18 February 1916. Lyrics to his musical effort were attributed to Carl Copeland.

In 1925, two years before the Fishback printing, Texas folklorist J. Frank Dobie came across two lines of the song in an unpublished manuscript by Andy Adams, acknowledged as probably the most faithful author who ever lived the life of a cowboy and wrote about it. Through correspondence with the trail driver, Dobie was able to learn that Adams had been familiar with the song for a number of years, was responsible for parts of the second stanza, and had actually written a third stanza to the song. The Adams source for fragments of the song was an old-time Texas ranchman.

In addition to wanting to be in Texas for the spring roundup, Adams reveals another reason for his wanting to return:

There's a grave in sunny Texas where Mollie
    Deming sleeps,
'Mid a grove of mossy liveoaks that constant
    vigil keeps.
In my heart's a recollection of a long, long by-
    gone day
When we rode the range together like truant
    kids astray.
Her gentle spirit calls me in the watches of the
    night,
And I hear her laughter freshening the dew of
    early light.
Yes, I was foreman of that cow ranch—the
    calling of a king,
And I'd like to be in Texas when they round up
    in the spring.*

Calumet Music Company of Chicago published the song in the public domain in 1935 under a slightly different title, "I'd Like To Be in Texas For the Round Up in the Spring." However, two years later in a revised edition the name of the song was corrected, Williams and Copeland were restored as composers, and Fishback was credited with the

*J. Frank Dobie, "Ballads and Songs of the Frontier Folk," *Publications of the Texas Folk-Lore Society*, no. 6 (1927): 161–63.

Lon Fishback (Courtesy of
Lon Fishback, Jr.)

Andy Adams (By permission
of Western History Collections, University of Oklahoma
Library)

original copyright (although his first name was in-
correctly spelled Lou).

Calumet Music Company was a subsidiary of the
M. M. Cole Publishing Company of Chicago. Both
companies were founded by Maurice M. Cole, a
native of New York who later became associated
with Sears, Roebuck and Company of Chicago as a
part of his product merchandising. Cole was a
close friend of Gene Autry, who was then a radio
performer on WLS Chicago. With the help of Autry
and other western performers, Cole published
cowboy songs in the public domain through his

affiliate company. His sheet music sold for five
cents or less during the Great Depression, and the
publishing house actually made a profit through
the hard times by using demo-piano promotion in
dime stores.

Evidence that a form of "I'd Like to Be in Texas
When They Round Up in the Spring" is a traditional song that was in oral circulation long before
it was published by Fishback was given by another
source of J. Frank Dobie. His close friend W. W.
Burton, who was from a Texas family of ranchers,
rangers, freighters, farmers, prospectors, and hunt-

ers, claimed to have heard the song in the 1880s in the young town of Colorado City, Texas. But it was promoter Lon Fishback, who died in California on 27 October 1963, who brought the song to the attention of widespread American audiences.

I'd Like to Be in Texas When They Round Up in the Spring

oth-ers New Or-leans. In a cor-ner in an old armed chair, sat a man whose hair was
quiet-ly thus be - gan I've seen them stampede o'er the hills un - til you'd think they'd nev - er

gray.   He list-ened to them eag-er-ly to what they had to say. They
stop.   I've seen them run for miles and miles un - til the lead-er dropped. I was

asked him where he'd like to be, His clear old voice did ring.   I'd
fore - man on a ranch the call-ing of a king.   I'd

like to be in Tex - as, When they round up in the spring.
like to be in Tex - as for the round up in the spring.

7 Sierra Sue 1916

It was in 1913 that Joseph Buell Carey moved to San Francisco from Eureka, California, to compose popular songs and form the Buell Music Company—nothing unusual except that only three years before Joe Carey was left totally blind following an accident involving his motorcycle and an automobile.

During the forty years preceding his misfortune Carey had a varied career. He played in honky-tonk saloons during the Klondike gold rush of 1898, returned to Eureka where he sold pianos and had a music store, was organist and choirmaster in the Episcopal church, and was a director of the Conservatory of Music in Portland, Oregon. He also directed bands, plays, orchestras, and musicals at the same time he was composing high-quality songs, hymns, and an opera that was never finished.

Joe Carey was born on 24 May 1871 in Dixon, California, within sight of the High Sierras, and he spent much time in the mountains. It was his early memory of the trails, the rocks and rills, and the cooing of gentle doves that inspired the blind composer to write and publish "Sierra Sue" in 1916, six years after his near fatal accident. The composition, subtitled "A Song of the Hills," was rediscovered in 1939 by Bing Crosby, who heard it played at a piano bar, traced down its source, and recorded it. Shapiro, Bernstein & Company bought the copyright a year later and became publisher of the song. For fourteen weeks "Sierra Sue" was on the radio show "Your Hit Parade" as one of the most popular songs in the United States. On 17 August 1940, it was introduced as the number 1 hit song in the nation, one of the very few revival songs to make the top spot.

"Your Hit Parade" is probably the most celebrated early radio program in the history of American popular music. Based on sheet music and record sales throughout the country and on the number of radio and dance band performances, the weekly Saturday night program featured the top songs of the week, varying in numbers over the years between five and fifteen. The show was first aired on 20 July 1935, and made its first television appearance on 10 July 1950. All programming ended on 7 June 1958.

Gene Autry featured "Sierra Sue" in his 1941 Republic movie *Sierra Sue*, co-starring Fay McKenzie and comic sidekick George "Gabby" Hayes.

Joseph B. Carey, the master ballad writer, composed a number of songs having worldwide interest. His Hawaiian song "She Sang 'Aloha' to Me" won international fame. Another global gem was his "Zanzibar," and lovers of Irish songs found his heart-gripping ballad "The Colleen Who Waits for Me" particularly appealing.

Those who knew the blind composer, and the thousands who attended Carey concerts during his later life, found another lasting influence in Joe Carey's character. Unaware that he was doing so, he gave lesson after lesson in courage as audiences marveled at his ability to turn misfortune into fortune, despair into happiness, and grief into mirth.

Joseph Buell Carey (Courtesy of Buell Carey Ellis)

Although he lived in darkness after the loss of his eyesight at age forty, his music still reflected the sunshine of his soul when he died in San Francisco on 3 October 1930, ten years before his "Sierra Sue" became a nationwide favorite.*

*Morris DeH. Tracy, "Joseph Carey Teaches Great Lesson of Life," Eureka (Calif.) *Daily Humboldt Standard*, 29 January 1913.

Sierra Sue

By the Composer of She "Sang 'Aloha' to Me"

Words and Music by
JOSEPH B. CAREY.

Far from the cit - y of sor - rows, Sweet - heart I'm wait - ing for
Some day you'll tire of the cit - y, Then you'll re - turn to the

you _____ Come to the hills that love you,
fold _____ Far down the trail I'll meet you,

CHORUS.

Come to a heart fond and true ____
Lov-ing and true as of old ____ Si-er-ra Sue ____ I'm sad and

lone-ly ____ The rocks and rills ____ are sigh-ing too ____ Si-er-ra

Sue ____ I want you on-ly ____ No one but you ____ Si-er-ra

Sue ___ The ro-ses droop ___ their heads in sad - ness ___ The gen -tle

doves ___ no long-er coo ___ Ah can't you hear ___ my sad heart

call - ing ___ Call -ing for you ___ Si - er - ra Sue. ___

8 Let the Rest of The World Go By 1919

Extensive promotion by performer, composer, publisher, and record company is essential for the success of a song. When "Let the Rest of The World Go By" was written in 1919, Tin Pan Alley was a beehive of promotional activity. Without the advantage of overnight nationwide exposure brought about later through radio and television media, early composers had to promote a new song to a publisher personally. Once the song was accepted, the publisher would sometimes hire teams of roving musicians to plug it through performances in dance halls, theaters, and stores. The best way to ensure its success was to have a big star introduce it in a musical show.

"Let the Rest of The World Go By" is the tuneful reflection of a discontented city dweller who yearns to get away from the everyday humdrum of life and find peace and happiness somewhere in the West with a true love. Ernest R. Ball wrote the music and J. Keirn Brennan the lyrics.

Ball, who was born in Cleveland, Ohio, on 21 July 1878, gained international fame as a composer of Irish songs. Showing a remarkable aptitude for music at an early age, Ball began giving music lessons at thirteen. His first composition was a march written when he was fifteen. While still a young man, Ball traveled to New York City and became a relief pianist at the Union Square Theatre and later a demonstrator for music publishers M. Witmark & Sons. He remained with the firm through a twenty-year contract and died during a ten-year renewal.

Ernest R. Ball (ASCAP)

In addition to other successes, Ball's great Irish classics include "Mother Machree," "When Irish Eyes Are Smiling," "Ireland Is Ireland to Me," "That's How the Shannon Flows," and his last song, "Rose of Killarney." Ball died of a heart attack in his dressing room following a performance in Santa Ana, California, on 3 May 1927.

J. Keirn Brennan, poet and lyricist, was a native Californian, born in San Francisco on 24 November 1873. Following a youthful career as a cowpuncher in Texas and a gold rusher in the Klon-

J. Keirn Brennan (Courtesy of
Ann Brown)

dike, Brennan became a professional singer for a
Chicago publishing house before moving on to Tin
Pan Alley.

Brennan began collaborating with Ball in 1914
with their Irish classic "A Little Bit of Heaven." In
subsequent years they shared honors for "Good-
bye, Good Luck, God Bless You," "Turn Back the
Universe (and Give Me Yesterday)," "Ireland Is
Ireland to Me," "In the Garden of the Gods," and
"If It Takes a Thousand Years." Their great tri-
umph came in 1919 with "Let the Rest of The
World Go By."

Even though Ball and Brennan were well established in the songwriting field and the song was
destined to become a popular standard, "Let the
Rest of The World Go By" would not have made it
except for the unshaken confidence of one member
of a large publishing family.

M. Witmark & Sons had accepted "Let the Rest
of The World Go By," but early sales were dis-
couraging. Numerous sessions were held by the
music company executives to discuss dropping the
song in favor of others. It appeared to be doomed.
But Julius Witmark believed in the song and insisted on intensified promotion. "Let the Rest of
The World Go By" was subsequently pushed to
sheet music sales totaling 3.5 million copies.
Years later it achieved promotional heights in the
1944 Ernest R. Ball screen biography, *When Irish
Eyes Are Smiling*, when popular vocalist Dick
Haynes, supported by a male chorus, reintroduced
the song.*

Ernest R. Ball dedicated "Let the Rest of The
World Go By" to his close associates "Julie and
Carrie," Julius Witmark and Carrie Northey (nei-
ther of whom ever married). Northey, whose professional name was Caro Roma, was a successful
songwriter who collaborated with Ball on a number
of song hits and was affiliated with M. Witmark &
Sons for half a century.

*Isadore Widmark and Isaac Goldberg, *From Ragtime to Swing-
time* (New York: Lee Furman, Inc., 1939), 339–45.

To Julie and Carrie

Let The Rest Of The World Go By

Words by
J. KEIRN BRENNAN

Music by
ERNEST R. BALL

just run a - way, Out where the west winds call._____
won - der - ful West, A - cross the great Di - vide?_____

REFRAIN *Tenderly with expression*

With some one like you, a pal good and true, I'd like to leave it

all be - hind, and go and find Some place that's known to God a -

9

When It's Springtime
In the Rockies 1923

During many years of nationwide popularity, "When It's Springtime In the Rockies" became known as the national song of the West, and its composer once even introduced it to an audience, either accidently or by design, as the national anthem!

Mary Hale was a lovely, cherubic-faced girl in a sixth-grade Utah classroom when she began to write poetry. While still a high school student in 1915, she wrote the words to "When It's Springtime In the Rockies."

A youthful Mary Hale Woolsey about the time she wrote the song lyrics to "When It's Springtime In the Rockies." (Courtesy of Lael Woolsey Hill)

Professor Robert Sauer (Brigham Young University Archives)

Mary Elizabeth Hale was born in Spanish Fork, Utah, on 21 March 1899, but she grew up in Provo below the towering summits of the Rocky Mountains. As a youthful romanticist, Hale depicted in verse the longing she imagined she would feel if ever forced to be apart from her beloved mountains and a prince charming of her dreams for any length of time. Year after year she had seen the transforming of long cold winters into blue-eyed springs, and it worked magic in her heart. The result was a poetic dream of springtime and the happy reunion with a sweetheart.

Hale took her lyrics to Robert Sauer, band director at Brigham Young University, for a possible musical adaptation. Unimpressed, he put the sheet of paper in his desk and forgot about it.

Years went by. Hale married, adding Woolsey to her name. One day in 1923 Professor Sauer came across the unsigned paper in his office. This time he liked the words, and he added music, borrowing the melody of an old German folk song. He copyrighted "When It's Springtime In the Rockies" and published it himself the same year. Professor Sauer invented the name T. Snow that appeared as lyricist with his on the original sheet music.

Sauer was born in Rammeneau, Saxony, Germany, on 3 October 1872. Through the influence of Brigham Young University band leader Albert Miller, Sauer joined the Mormon Church in Germany in 1899. He moved to Provo, Utah, in 1905, and a year later became the director of the BYU band.

When Mary Hale Woolsey eventually heard her words to "When It's Springtime In the Rockies" being sung, she hastened to Sauer with her original copy and quickly convinced him that she was the source of the song's words. Sauer drew up a contract giving Woolsey due credit for any future printings of the song.*

The song originally had only minimal exposure. Then radio came to Salt Lake City. The station manager of KSL liked "When It's Springtime In the Rockies" and presented it regularly on the sta-

*Harrison R. Merrill, "When It's Springtime in the Rockies," Salt Lake City (Utah) *Deseret News*, 10 February 1934.

tion. In 1928 a local singing duo known as Bob and Monte changed the Sauer tempo and recorded the song on Vocalion Records.

In the meantime Milt Taggart, a local bandleader and department head in a Salt Lake City music store, plugged the song on radio. Believing that with the right promotion it would become a national hit, Taggart got in touch with Sauer and Woolsey and worked out a contract authorizing him to sell the song for a portion of its proceeds. In 1929 the San Francisco music publishing firm of Villa Morét printed the song with Milt Taggart identified as co-writer of the music. In a later edition, this acknowledgment was withdrawn and he was listed as co-author of the words. Subsequently his name was removed from all credits.

Professor Sauer died in Provo, Utah, on 5 January 1944, and Mary Hale Woosley died in Santa Monica, California, on 6 December 1969. Their "When It's Springtime In the Rockies" lives on as one of the most beloved songs of the American West.

When It's Springtime In the Rockies
A Charming Waltz Song

Words by
MARY HALE WOOLSEY

Music by
ROBERT SAUER
& MILT TAGGART

Tempo di Valse (*Dreamily*)

The twi - light shad - ows deep - en in - to night, dear;
I've kept your im - age guard - ed in my heart, dear;

The cit - y lights are gleam - ing o'er the snow;
I've kept my love, for you, as pure as dew;

I sit a - lone be - side the cheer - y fire, dear; I'm
I'm long - ing for the time when I shall come, dear; Back

10 Mexicali Rose
1923

Orchestra leader Jack Tenney wrote "Mexicali Rose" in 1923. At the time he was filling an engagement at the Owl, a landmark cabaret in Mexicali, Mexico, reputed to have the longest bar in the world. Partly because of Prohibition in the United States, Mexicali had become a tourist mecca for gamblers, drinkers, and, some say, for all the vices of humanity. About the time Prohibition ended in the United States, the old Owl burned to the ground and Mexicali settled back down to the typical border town it once had been.

"Mexicali Rose" is just one of the many songs Tenney wrote for the revues at the Owl. He wrote the music first, and, while he was groping for words, a Mexican janitress was in the background, quietly going about her morning cleaning. Her name was Rose. As Tenney watched her, the name Mexicali Rose came to his mind and a song was born. As he put it, the rest of the song wrote itself.

Encouraged by the popularity of the song in Mexico, Tenney sent it to publisher after publisher, but each one rejected it. Some time later an appreciative California music lover, Helen Stone, heard the song and offered to publish it with her own money. For this assistance, Tenney gave her credit for the words. The copyright to the yet-unsuccessful song was sold for a pittance in 1935 to M. M. Cole Publishing Company. It soon became a worldwide hit and was eventually translated into sixteen languages.

Jack Breckenridge Tenney sold almost one hundred songs and was said to have composed another

Jack Tenney (California State Library)

four hundred that were never placed on the market, but he always insisted that songwriting was a hobby.

Born on 1 April 1898 in St. Louis, Missouri, Tenney moved to California at the age of ten. He served in World War I and in the 1920s played the organ in theaters in San Francisco and Los Angeles. It was also in the 1920s that he organized his own dance band. In 1919 Tenney became a member of Local 47 of the American Federation of

Musicians in Los Angeles. He went on to organize and become the first president of the Las Vegas local.

Jack Tenney later became a prominent Los Angeles attorney. He entered politics in 1936 with his election to the California State Assembly from the 46th District, which encompassed southwest Los Angeles and Catalina Island. He was reelected in 1938 and 1940. In 1942 he was elected to the California Senate. Tenney ran for the U.S. Senate in 1944 but was defeated in the primary. Two years later he again became a state senator. He had the honor of running for vice president of the United States in 1952 with presidential nominee General Douglas MacArthur on the Christian Nationalist Party ticket and was on the ballot in sixteen states.

Jack Tenney was well liked by his fellow legislators, and his ability to play the piano put him in great demand as an entertainer at legislative functions. Invariably, he was called upon to play "Mexicali Rose."

Shortly before his death on 4 November 1970 in Glendale, California, Jack Tenney was the guest of the governor of Baja California and the mayor of Mexicali, both of whom met him at the border with a long parade of Mexican dignitaries and musicians to welcome and honor him as the person who put Mexicali on the map.

Tune Ukulele or
Banjo with Piano
G C E A

Brunswick Record No. 2649
Vocalion   ʺ   ʺ 14763
Victor   ʺ   ʺ 77255
Okeh   ʺ   ʺ 4952
Q. R. S. Word Roll ʺ 2669

MEXICALI ROSE
(MEXICALI ROSA)

Also Published For:

ORCH. (small) . 25¢ net
ORCH. (full) . . 35¢ net
FULL BAND . 50¢ net

Spanish Translation by
Manuel Sanchez De Lara

Words by
HELEN STONE

Ukulele and Banjo Chords
by Frank Littig

Music by
JACK B. TENNEY

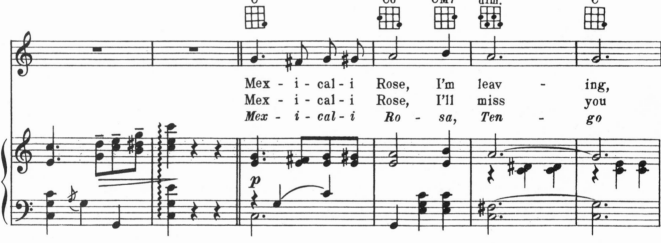

Mex - i - cal - i Rose, I'm leav - ing,
Mex - i - cal - i Rose, I'll miss you
Mex - i - cal - i Ro - sa, Ten - go

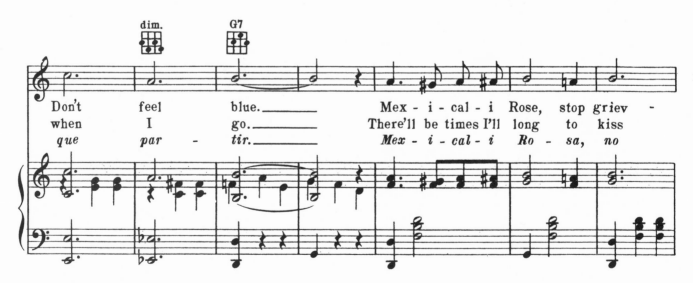

Don't feel blue._____ Mex - i - cal - i Rose, stop griev -
when I go._____ There'll be times I'll long to kiss
que par - tir._____ Mex - i - cal - i Ro - sa, no

11 The Utah Trail
1928

The composer of "The Utah Trail" was born Robert Palmer White in Illinois on 19 September 1897, but he shortened the name to Bob Palmer for his professional career.

Beginning at an early age, the future songwriter played vaudeville, summer stock, and road shows throughout the Midwest circuit. His career was interrupted when he enlisted in the armed forces during World War I and served overseas. By the time he returned home and went through a period of hospitalization, radio had opened a new field of entertainment and Palmer played out of the San Francisco and West Coast circuits.

In the late 1920s, Bob Palmer had his own radio show on KSL in Salt Lake City. While there he wrote and introduced his own composition, "The Utah Trail," and made the first radio broadcast of another romantic Utah song, "When It's Springtime In the Rockies." While in Salt Lake City, Palmer also filled in as a clarinetist in the Fort Douglas Band.

The setting Palmer used for "The Utah Trail" was the Mormon road through Emigration Canyon. On 20 July 1847 advance scouts for the initial party of Saints stood on a ridge above the canyon and beheld the view that would move an ailing Brigham Young four days later to declare, in essence, "This is the Place!" Spread before the Mormons was one of the most beautiful vistas in America, their long-anticipated Promised Land.

Bob Palmer left Utah to become the introductory act for the successful postwar play *What Price Glory?* on the Orpheum circuit in Los Angeles and the Pantages Theatres. He teamed up with a fellow entertainer, Monte Hall, and they billed themselves "The Song Birds of the Golden West." (Hall was not the Monte Hall of later television game show fame.)

Bob and Monte recorded "The Utah Trail" and "When It's Springtime In the Rockies" for Vocalion Records in 1928. Monte left the team two years later and the singing duet became Bob and Jimmy, with Jimmy Palmer making it a brother act. He had previously played guitar background on the Bob and Monte radio programs.

Bob Palmer founded the Robert Palmer Publishing Company in Los Angeles and published "The Utah Trail" in 1928. Other personal songs published by him include "An Old Fashioned Sweetheart of Mine," "From the Heart of the West Came You," "Pals," "Where the Golden Poppies Grow," "That Tumbled Down Shack in Dixieland," and "Spread a Smile."

Additional popularity for "The Utah Trail" came in 1928 when Southern Music Publishing Company secured the copyright, printed it in sheet music form, and included it in *The Carter Family Album of Smokey Mountain Ballads*. Even though the setting for the origin of the song implied by the folio title is grossly inaccurate, its inclusion in the collection gave additional nationwide exposure to "The Utah Trail." It was featured in the 1945

motion picture *Utah*, starring Roy Rogers, Dale Evans, and Gabby Hayes.

After his retirement, Bob Palmer moved to Lodi, California, and became active in a senior citizens' orchestra of former professionals. He died in Lodi on 1 July 1982.

The Utah Trail

Words and Music by
"BOB" PALMER

Moderato

You ask me where I'm go - in'   So ear - ly in the
The crim - son sky of Au - tumn,   The fra - grant breath of

dawn.   I'm just a trav' - ler rov - ing,
spring,   Will lin - ger on for ev - er,

Just a roam - in'   on   I've looked this   old   world
Fond-est mem - ries   bring.   When   as   a   boy   I

o - ver,   Man-y   times have search'd in   vain _____ For   a   spot that seems like
wan-dered To the hills and swim-min' holes _____Watched at   ev - en tide the

heav - en   to   me ___   And I   long to   be   a - gain.
set - ing   sun ___ Turn the   lakes deep blue   to   gold.

CHORUS

I'm goin' to hide a-way Out be - side the U - tah trail.

Moon - light as bright as day Far out on that U - tah trail

There's where I'll set - tle down in peace where all is still ____ In a

lit-tle hut just built for two Tuck'd a - way in the heart of the hills.

There 'neath the skies of blue In the gold-en sum-mer time;

Out where all friends are true And all nat-ure is in rhyme.

Some - one is wait-ing With a love that nev-er fails. —— Wait - ing

pa-tient-ly to wel-come me Far out on that U-tah trail. trail. ——

12 Goin' Back To Texas
1929

Carson J. Robison was a pioneer songwriter, radio entertainer, and recording artist in the world of country and western music. In America he was affectionately known as "the granddaddy of the hillbillies," and he was billed as "radio's hillbilly king" while performing in England. Robison began his career in both radio and records in the early 1920s. His recording were popular not only in America; their heavy sales in England, Australia, Canada, South Africa, and other foreign countries brought him international fame.

Carson Jay Robison was born in Oswego, Kansas, on 4 August 1890, and he was raised in Chetopa, a small village south of Oswego near the Oklahoma border. His father was a champion cowboy fiddler and dance-caller, so music was a part of Robison's early life. As a youth he developed the art of whistling two tones at once in harmony. He also learned to play the guitar and harmonica at the same time by using a wire neck frame to hold the mouth organ. His whistling was to bring him his first big break in the entertainment field.

When he was old enough, Robison turned to railroading, but the thunder of locomotives made him long for distant cities, and songs-to-be were forever buzzing around in his head. He moved on to working in the oil industry. Then, in 1920, he left the colorful Oklahoma and Texas oil fields for Kansas City, Missouri, to begin his professional career in music. When radio station WDAF went on the air, Robison was hired as one of their first singing performers.

Wendall Hall, a fellow Kansan who had achieved success in New York as an entertainer and composer of the novelty hit "It Ain't Gonna Rain No Mo," met Robison in Kansas City. He was impressed by the double-tone whistle of the young man and encouraged him to go to New York. Robison made the move to the big city in 1924 and whistled his way into big time and big records with his recordings of "Songbirds in Georgia" and "Whistle Your Blues Away."

Robison arrived in New York with $3.65 in his pockets, frayed clothes, and a hat that looked like it had been snitched from a hobo. He hired a taxi to the "gramophone studios," where he was given a two-year contract and paid $20 in advance. He split this up and repaid four dollars each to five fellows from whom he had borrowed money. He walked the streets at night and went hungry for days.

Once established in New York in radio and recordings, Robison broadcast everything from "a panther's scream upwards," as he once said. Current events inspired a number of his early compositions. When big news stories were broadcast over radio, he put his thoughts into words and music. Song material included the airship *Shenandoah* disaster in Ohio in 1925, the devastating Miami hurricane in 1926, the sinking of the steamship *Vestris* off the Virginia Capes in 1928, and the state prison fire in Ohio that killed more than three hundred inmates in 1930. Before the tragic Lindbergh kidnapping in 1932, Robison had welcomed

Carson J. Robison and Vernon Dalhart (Country Music Foundation Library and Music Center)

the birth of the child with the song "Hello Young Lindy!"

Robison recorded songs with fellow Kansan Frank Luther, who helped him write "Barnacle Bill the Sailor." It later became an orally circulated bawdy song with words other than those of the composers. He also made a number of records with Vernon Dalhart, an early recorder of traditional cowboy songs.

His early longing for cities reversed on Robison occasionally, for he began writing songs about going back to where he came from. In 1929 he wrote the cowboy standard "Goin' Back To Texas," paying homage to one of the states from which he started out to make himself a name.

Goin' Back To Texas

Words and Music
by
CARSON J. ROBISON

Victor Record No. V-40073

Moderato

13 When the Bloom Is On the Sage 1930

"When the Bloom Is On the Sage" was written by the Happy Chappies in 1930 during a radio broadcast of the Blue Monday Jamboree over KFRC in San Francisco, California. At the beginning of the show the program director received a wire from a rich Texan who offered $250 to the harmony team of Fred Howard and Nat Vincent if they could write a song and play it before the program ended.* They got to work.

Nat Vincent had the seed planted in his mind for a Texas song a number of years before when he was a guest at a cattle roundup near Fort Worth. One evening beside the campfire, Vincent began to have that certain feeling that cowboys have while drinking black coffee from an old tin can. Years later he described the scene: "You can't imagine how beautiful it was. The moon came up, flooding the sage with light that made a display of vivid blues and purple that is hard to describe."†

It was this feeling and setting that Vincent proposed to Howard when they got the offer to write a song while on the air. Howard was one of those rare lyricists who could come up with song words quickly when given an idea, a title, or a melody. Before the program ended, the two were playing and singing "When the Bloom Is On the Sage."

The Happy Chappies formed in 1926 in San Francisco with Nat Vincent one of the original members. Fred Howard joined him a few years later when Vincent's initial partner left the team. The two young entertainers became a popular radio duet on KFRC and became nationally known through their songwriting and Columbia recordings.

Following their radio and recording stint in San Francisco, the Happy Chappies moved to radio KFI in Los Angeles to write songs for the original "Beverly Hill Billies" radio show.

Nat Vincent was one of the first successful Tin Pan Alley songwriters. He was born Nathaniel Hawthorne Vincent in Kansas City, Missouri, on 6 November 1889. As a youth he was fascinated with brass bands and during play would high-step around playing Sousa marches by humming through a paper-covered comb. He later taught himself to play the piano. With writing songs his goal, Vincent moved to New York City in 1909 and spent his first night on a park bench. After only six months he sold his first song, "While Under the Jungle Moon," which he had originally written for a high school play back home, and before the year ended, he had seven songs in print.

Vincent wrote for publishers, Broadway shows, movies, radio, television, and audiences on the spot. The most notable song in which he had a part was "I'm Forever Blowing Bubbles." Three of the four collaborating songwriters on this song, Kendis, Brockman, and Vincent, combined their names to create the pseudonym Jean Kenbrovin. His part in the song and his sparkling personality earned Vincent the nickname "Bubbles."

*Dorothy Horstman, *Sing Your Heart Out, Country Boy* (New York: E. P. Dutton & Co., 1975), 307–8.
†Jack Lewis, "Rancho Ramblin's," Sunland, Tujunga, La Cresenda, Sun Valley (Calif.) *Record-Ledger*, 3 October 1974.

Fred Howard and Nat Vincent, the "Happy Chappies," in 1930. (Courtesy of Faith Vincent)

Frederick Howard Wright was born on 30 September 1896 in San Diego, California. For many years as an entertainer and songwriter he dropped his family name and became famous as Fred Howard. He had a talent for writing verse as a youngster, and his fine tenor voice soon earned him a place with a musical stock company in San Diego. In a short time he was producing his own musicals up and down the Pacific Coast and in Hawaii. From 1935 to 1940 he was a member of the "Ma Perkins" soap opera radio cast, playing the part of the family lawyer, D. Pemberton Toohey.

Fred Howard and Nat Vincent graced the songwriting field for many years. As late as the 1960s they were still writing "tailor-made" songs for individual artists. Nat Vincent died on 6 June 1979.

When the Bloom Is On the Sage

Tune Uke
G C E A
Arr. by Eddie Durant

Words & Music by
FRED HOWARD & NAT VINCENT

14 When It's Night-time in Nevada 1931

Statewide in setting but international in perspective, the cowboy love song "When It's Night-time in Nevada" was written by an Englishman, a Canadian, and an American midwesterner.

The three songwriters frequently got together at the Wurlitzer Music Store in Detroit, Michigan. Richard W. Pascoe was a poet who liked to rhyme and romanticize in music, H. O'Reilly Clint was a municipal employee and church organist, and Will E. Dulmage was a salesman in the music store.

Richard W. Pascoe was born on 5 December 1888 in Penzance, Cornwall, England, and came to the United States in 1907. Beginning in 1914, he started writing song lyrics and singing his songs throughout the Midwest to any audiences he could find from five- and ten-cent stores to Detroit radio stations. He died in Detroit on 23 December 1968.

H. O'Reilly Clint was from Smiths Falls, Ontario. Born on 20 September 1899, he was christened John Harold Clint, but everybody who knew him called him Harold. He attended Smiths Falls Collegiate Institute from 1914 to 1920 and was active in the school musicals. The young man then

Above: H. O'Reilly Clint in 1944. (Courtesy of Doris E. Cameron)

Left: Richard W. Pascoe (Courtesy of Frances M. Pascoe)

Will E. Dulmage (Courtesy of Bill Dulmage)

enrolled in the Toronto Conservatory of Music but soon moved to Detroit to work as an auditor in the city government. He dropped the name John and added the middle name O'Reilly, the maiden name of his mother.

Clint wrote songs for military, collegiate, and fraternal organizations, including the American Legion, the Veterans of Foreign Wars, the University of Michigan, the Elks, and the Knights of Columbus. He composed the University of Michigan alma mater even though he never attended a class there, and he wrote the music to "It's Detroit," adopted in 1951 as the official song for the 250th anniversary of that city. He helped form the Clint and Nagel Music Publishers in Detroit with Norman Nagel, a collaborator on a number of songs. Clint died in Detroit on 30 September 1961.

Will E. Dulmage, composer of popular and semi-classical music, was born on 17 August 1883 in Holly, Michigan. Dulmage was a staff member of a music publishing house in Detroit for twenty-one years before becoming a sheet music executive. He died on 11 February 1953 in Dearborn, Michigan.

Clint and Dulmage collaborated in 1931 to produce the music to "When It's Night-time in Nevada," turning to their friend Richard W. Pascoe for the words. Pascoe was a nature-loving man who became attuned to men riding the ranges and living alone under the stars with the beauty of campfires and Nevada nights. He traveled across the country a number of times, visiting along the way with storekeepers, restaurant employees, and any cowboy who happened by. His feelings for the western scene were incorporated in the song lyrics he created.

Roy Rogers sang "When It's Night-time in Nevada" along with traditional cowboy songs in the 1948 Republic production *Night Time in Nevada*.

"In My Heart There's a Part of the Prairie" is another western composition by Pascoe, Clint, and Dulmage.

When It's Night-time in Nevada

Tune Uke

A   D   F#   B

Lyric by
RICHARD W. PASCOE

Music by
WILL E. DULMAGE &
H. O'REILLY CLINT

15 The Last Round-Up
1931

The traditional spring roundup on the open range was a hunt to bring back cattle that had scattered and mingled with those of other owners during the summer, autumn, and winter months. Sections of the range were designated for the convenience of hunting cattle and rounding them up. Riding the perimeter of each section was a squad of two or three cowboys who crossed and recrossed the area, gradually accumulating a herd of cattle that had grown sullen and obstinate through lack of human contact. These cattle were driven back to merge with the herds rounded up from other sections. Then came the wearisome task of cutting the writhing mass of cattle, separating and regrouping all those carrying the same brands.

For the cowboy himself, to be "rounded up in glory" was sometimes the result of his last earthly roundup. Seemingly oblivious to the steep grades, treacherous holes, and fallen trees, cowboys were close to death time and time again in their wild pursuit of cattle.

Aspiring songwriters Billy Hill and Nat Vincent were visitors on a Texas ranch during roundup time in the mid-1920s. From a vantage point on a knoll overlooking a scene of hazardous activity, they witnessed a cowboy being trampled to death after falling from his horse. The memory of the tragedy later inspired Hill to write "The Last Round-Up."

George Hill, father of Billy Hill, was one-half Blackfoot Indian. He spent most of his life roaming around the West, sailing the seven seas, going around Cape Horn several times, and spending time in Alaska. While in the port of Boston he met a Latvian peasant girl, and they were married. Their son, William Joseph Hill, was born in the Boston suburb of Jamaica Plain on 14 July 1899.

Billy Hill studied violin in the New England Conservatory but headed west when he was only seventeen years old. He worked as a cowboy in Montana and a laborer in the Death Valley mines,

Billy Hill (Courtesy of Lee DeDette Taylor)

and he washed dishes in roadhouses to finance his wanderings. He lingered long enough in Salt Lake City to organize a jazz band for a local Chinese restaurant and made a tour of Nevada, Idaho, Montana, and Hawaii.

In Hollywood, Billy Hill wrote film scores for MGM, Paramount, and Columbia. On the day he left to go back to the East Coast in 1930, he married DeDette Walker, the beautiful showgirl who had posed for the statue that became "The Columbia Lady" logo for Columbia Pictures, and they headed east for Tin Pan Alley.

Just outside Yuma, Arizona, the newlyweds had their fourth tire blowout of the day on an old Model T Ford and spent their wedding night in a ditch. Billy sat up most of the night and wrote a song, "The West, a Nest, and You," for his bride.

After moving to New York, the determined songwriter struggled to make a living working as a doorman for a Fifth Avenue apartment house. When he wrote "The Last Round-Up" in 1931, he had barely enough money to support himself and his wife. By the time their daughter was born in 1933 the couple was penniless, the rent was due, and the gas was turned off in their cold-water flat in Greenwich Village. While hospital authorities were refusing to admit DeDette until they were paid in advance to deliver her child, she gave birth to her daughter, Lee, in the elevator. The desperate father came close to selling "The Last Round-Up" outright to a phonograph company for $25 and would have done so if Gene Buck, president of the American Society of Composers, Authors, and Publishers, had not advanced a loan of $200 to help him through the hard times.* Shapiro, Bernstein & Company published the song in 1933, and Joe Morrison introduced it in the Paramount Theatre in New York. It was performed the following year by Don Ross in the *Ziegfeld Follies of 1934.*

When "The Last Round-Up" came out in 1933, commercial radio broadcasting was only thirteen years old, and home radios were becoming more available as America began to emerge from the Great Depression. Radio listening was becoming a national pastime, and "The Last Round-Up" quickly became a nationwide hit. The familiar refrain "git along, little dogie, git along, git along" could be heard daily over radio stations throughout the country. It remains one of the most popular cowboy songs ever written.

*Lee DeDette Hill Taylor, "Billy Hill Story" (Valencia, Calif., 1974), typescript, 10 pp.

THE LAST ROUND-UP

By BILLY HILL

Moderato *(not too fast)*

16 When The Cactus Is In Bloom 1931

Jimmie Rodgers, "America's Blue Yodeler" (Jimmie Rodgers Museum)

later adopted as his home as early as 1916, when he wrote his Aunt Dora from a railroad boarding-house in New Orleans that he was "going to Elpaso Texas in a weak or 10 days."[*]

In 1931 Jimmie Rodgers wrote "When The Cactus Is In Bloom," a song that had a substantial impact on the emerging singing-cowboy image in motion pictures and on records. His biographer, Nolan Porterfield, appraised the song:

> It is ersatz Western—a little more stylized, more "written" than older, more authentic songs of the range. But as a prototype, and a good one, "When The Cactus Is In Bloom" compares favorably with almost any of the sagebrush serenades later cranked out by celluloid wranglers gathered around the old campfire on Sound Stage 2B.[†]

James Charles Rodgers was born on 8 September 1897 in the rural community of Pine Springs, a few miles northeast of Meridian, Mississippi. As a kid Jimmie picked cotton by day and a guitar by

Jimmie Rodgers, "America's Blue Yodeler," wrote a song about Texas in 1929, calling it "The Land of My Boyhood Dreams." Three other songs, "Desert Blues," "Jimmie's Texas Blues," and "Yodeling Cowboy," inspired by the same state, were written and recorded the same year. Young Jimmie may have traveled to the state he

[*] Nolan Porterfield, "Stranger Through Your Town: The Background and Early Life of Jimmie Rodgers," *The John Edwards Memorial Foundation Quarterly* 8, no. 45 (Spring 1977): 14.
[†] Nolan Porterfield, *Jimmie Rodgers: The Life and Times of America's Blue Yodeler* (Urbana: University of Illinois Press, 1979), 295.

night. He won a talent show in Meridian and ran away with a medicine show at age thirteen. Returning home the following summer, Jimmy began to work with his father, a section foreman on the Mobile & Ohio Railroad. In December he became a railroad man, a short career handicapped by frequent colds, pleurisy, and other chest ailments.

By 1923 Jimmie Rodgers's life as a callboy, flagman, baggageman, and brakeman on the railroad was almost over. Recurring illnesses forced him to take temporary work. In the spring he joined a company of comedians, appearing between acts and singing songs that combined blues music with a yodel. He was called home later in the year because of the death of his second daughter. The following winter he spent looking for railroad jobs as far away as Arizona. In the spring of 1924 he returned home a sick man, diagnosed as having tuberculosis. By the end of the year his railroading days were over.

On the pretense of looking for railroad work, but more likely looking for a healthful climate, Rodgers moved to the mountain city of Asheville, North Carolina, in January 1927. There he helped organize a musical group called the Jimmie Rodgers Entertainers and began a regular three-times-a-week live show on WWNC in May, three months after the radio station went on the air.

On 4 August 1927, Jimmie Rodgers recorded two songs for the Victor Talking Machine Company in nearby Bristol, Tennessee, and his brief entertainment career was on its way. For the next six years, he was to record 111 songs that sold millions of copies and helped earn him recognition as "The Father of Country Music."

Rodgers's health, however, was slowly deteriorating. In the spring of 1929 he visited Kerrville, Texas, in the heart of the hill country, where a number of sanitoriums for the treatment of lung disorders were located. There he built his dream home and named it Blue Yodeler's Paradise.

"That old T.B.," as he called it, was killing Jimmie Rodgers. On 20 May 1933, he recorded "The Yodeling Ranger" in New York City during an ex-

tended recording session that was interrupted by days in which he could not get out of his hotel bed. The song had been written in 1931 by Ray Hall when Rodgers was given an honorary commission in the Texas Rangers. Jimmie Rodgers died six days later, on 26 May 1933 in his room at the Manger Hotel (later the Hotel Taft) after recording half of a scheduled twenty-four-song recording session.

"He certainly wasn't much of a musician—couldn't read a note, keep time, play the 'right' chords, or write lyrics that fit," wrote his biographer. "All he could do was reach the hearts of millions of people around the world, and lift them up."*

Jimmie Rodgers was installed posthumously as the first member of the Country Music Hall of Fame in Nashville, Tennessee, on 3 November 1961 and honored as "the man who started it all."

*Porterfield, *Jimmie Rodgers: The Life and Times of America's Blue Yodeler*, 5.

When The Cactus Is In Bloom

Victor Record No. 23636

By JIMMIE RODGERS

The cat-tle prowled and the coyotes howled Out on that Great Di-vide.___ I nev-er
We don't have cold weath-er,___ It nev-er snows or rains.___

done no wrong, just sing-ing a song, As down the trail I ride.
That is where the sun-shines best, Out on the west-ern plains.

Rat-tle snakes rat-tle at the prai-rie dogs, You hear that mourn-ful tune.___ } It's
Some of the boys_ have_ gone a-way_ But they will be_ back soon.___

round up time_ a-way out West_ When the cac-tus is ___ in bloom.

17 Texas Plains
1932

"Texas Plains" was first recorded on 3 August 1934 in Hollywood, California, by Stuart Hamblen and His Covered Wagon Jubilee. Hamblen had written the song soon after his arrival in California to express his loneliness and his longing to go back to his beloved Texas plains where he could have his own saddle horse. It became his theme song for twenty-three years.

Carl Stuart Hamblen was one of the early great songwriting talents in country and western music to invade the Hollywood scene. He was born on 20 October 1908 in Kellyville, a small Marion County community in East Texas centered around the Kelly Plow Company that died when the pioneer plowshop was moved.

The son of an itinerant preacher, Stuart Hamblen lived in one small Texas town after another. He was educated to be a teacher, but the songs he heard while picking cotton with blacks inspired him to pursue a musical career. The traditional cowboy songs that he heard while doing general ranch work around Clarendon further influenced his future. In 1925 Hamblen started playing the guitar and singing over the radio in Dallas and Fort Worth as "Cowboy Joe from Abilene."

Loading his guitar and his dog, Shep, into an old Model T Ford in 1929, Hamblen drove to Camden, New Jersey, and through talent, gall, and persistence talked recording executives into letting him make three records for the Victor Talking Machine Company.

By early 1930 Hamblen was in Hollywood, where

Stuart Hamblen (Saturday Matinee)

he believed the greatest opportunity in a musical career awaited him. He joined the Beverly Hill Billies, the most popular country music group in southern California, but illness forced him to take a leave of absence. By the time he recovered, he had been replaced.

Later in 1930 Stuart Hamblen organized his own group, which included songstress Patsy Montana, and began a regular radio program on KMIC Inglewood. Two years later he secured the sponsorship of a local clothier, the Star Outfitting Company, and began an association that lasted twenty-two years. Intermittently, his group was known as the Lucky Stars.

During his career, Stuart Hamblen appeared as a supporting actor in numerous western movies. He also became heavily involved in training racehorses at Santa Anita, and he kept a pack of trail hounds for hunting mountain lions. In addition to the love songs inspired by his wife, Suzy, Hamblen wrote songs that tended to reflect the wild side of life. But in 1949 a big change occurred in both his life and his songs when he attended a tent revival held by evangelist Billy Graham. Hamblen became a Christian that night, and the new focus of his talent resulted in some of the finest gospel songs ever written. One night in 1950, at the home of John Wayne, his host casually remarked that it was no secret what God could do for a person. The comment struck a chord in the mind of Stuart Hamblen. When he got home he began writing as the clock chimed midnight. Fifteen minutes later, he had completed "It Is No Secret."*

The ever-busy Hamblen ran for president of the United States on the Prohibition party ticket in 1952, later remarking that Eisenhower beat him by only 24 million votes.

His chance finding of a dead prospector in an old cabin during one of his mountain lion hunts inspired one of Hamblen's greatest compositions, "This Old House." Although he wrote it as a sen-

sitive song, it was the upbeat tempo recording of it by Rosemary Clooney in 1954 that became a nationwide hit.

Soon after "Texas Plains" was written in 1932 the song was being passed along orally by western singers. Patsy Montana altered the title to "Montana Plains" the following year and introduced it as such on "National Barn Dance" over WLS Chicago. Folksinger Katie Lee of Arizona heard it over a radio station in Prescott in the 1930s as "The Western Plains."* Many early radio singers added their own special yodel.

Stuart Hamblen died on 8 March 1989 in the St. Johns Hospital and Health Center in Santa Monica, California, following brain surgery for a malignant tumor.

*Katie Lee, *Ten Thousand Goddam Cattle* (Flagstaff Ariz.: Northland Press, 1976), 6–7, 235–36.

*Ken Griffis, "I've Got So Many Million Years: The Story of Stuart Hamblen," *The John Edwards Memorial Foundation Quarterly* 14, no. 49 (Spring 1978): 4.

TEXAS PLAINS

Words & Music by
STUART HAMBLEN

18 Tumbling Tumbleweeds
1932

Bob Nolan was confined to his apartment in West Los Angeles, California, one November afternoon in 1932 because of rain. He worked as a caddy at the Bel Air Country Club, but the weather was too wet and windy for golf. While Bob stood there and stared out a window, leaves from the trees were being tumbled along the street by gusty winds. It was this bleak scene, and the sense of being confined, that inspired him to write a song he called "Tumbling Leaves."

After Nolan had performed his new song several times over the radio the following year, he began to get requests from audiences to sing about what they perceived to be "tumblin' weeds." He altered the tune to his song, added extra syllables, changed the herbage, and retitled it "Tumbling Tumbleweeds." Like the freedom of the barbed nomadic weed breaking away from its roots, wanderlust was an important factor in Bob Nolan's life. It was in this spirit that he produced some of the greatest of all western songs.

The celebrated Bob Nolan of cowboy and western music was born Robert Clarence Nobles in the isolated wilds of the Canadian province of New Brunswick on 1 April 1908. His father enlisted in the U.S. Army and was assigned to foreign service with the Royal Air Force during World War I. When the war was over, the elder Nobles moved to the dry desert climate near Tucson, Arizona, to restore his health. He arbitrarily changed his surname to Nolan because it sounded more American to him.

Bob Nolan excelled in track and field sports at Tucson High School and at the same time began writing poetry. He became a drifter in 1927 and explored the West, often hopping freight trains. In 1929 he joined a Chautauqua troupe and began a musical conversion of some of his poems, but the traveling tent work was not steady. His next job was that of a lifeguard on the beach at Venice, California.*

Still drawn to music, in 1931 Bob successfully auditioned for a musical singing group, the Rocky Mountaineers, after answering an ad placed in a Los Angeles newspaper by a young transplanted Ohioan named Leonard Slye, who later rode to fame as Roy Rogers. The group played and sang on radio station KGER in Long Beach, but Bob drifted from the pioneer harmony team in the fall of 1932. After finding work at the Bel Air, he continued writing songs and poems. Then came that memorable day when he watched the tumbling leaves from an apartment window.

"Tumbling Tumbleweeds" was not published until May 1934 by Sunset Music Company in Los Angeles. The publishing rights were quickly acquired by the Sam Fox Publishing Company in Cleveland, Ohio. The new edition by the larger company appeared only seven weeks after the original, but the song was slightly altered. Someone had rewritten Nolan's prelude to the refrain, turning it into one

*Kenneth J. Bindas, "Western Mystic: Bob Nolan and His Songs," *Western Historical Quarterly* 17, no. 4 (October 1986): 439.

for which he held little fondness, preferring his own personal assessment of being lonely but free as it was first published:

> Days may be dreary
> Still I'm not weary,
> My heart needs no consoling,
> At each break of dawn
> You'll find that I've gone
> Like old tumble weeds, I'm rolling.*

This philosophical statement is a more typical expression from the soul of the free-spirited Nolan about his propensity for drifting along.

*Larry Swisohn, "'Tumbling Tumble Weeds' Rediscovered," *Pioneer News* 1, no. 2 (May–June 1978): 5.

The Sons of the Pioneers as the O'Keefe Brothers in the Turquoise City Jail in *The Old Corral*, starring Gene Autry (Republic, 1936). *Left to right:* Hugh Farr, Bob Nolan, Tim Spencer, Len Slye (Roy Rogers), Karl Farr.

Tumbling Tumbleweeds

Words and Music by
BOB NOLAN

19
Carry Me Back To The Lone Prairie 1933

Internationally known songwriter and cowboy singer Carson J. Robison organized his own show troupe in 1932, calling it Carson Robison and the Buckaroos. The group—composed of Robison, John Mitchell, Bill Mitchell, and his wife, Pearl Pickens Mitchell—toured the United States and appeared regularly on coast-to-coast radio networks. Included in their repertory were original cowboy, country, religious, and humorous songs by Robison that have since become standards. They include songs like "Sleepy Rio Grande," "There's a Bridle Hangin' on the Wall," "Way Out West in Kansas," "In the Cumberland Mountains," "Left My Gal in the Mountains," "Carry Me Back to the Mountains," "My Blue Ridge Mountain Home," "Down on the Old Plantation," "Little Green Valley," "New River Train," and "I'm Going Back to Whur I Came From."

Changing their name to Carson Robison and the Pioneers, the western band toured the British Isles and performed for King George VI and Queen Elizabeth in the mid-1930s. By popular request they returned overseas in 1938 for their own fifteen- and thirty-minute shows over radio stations in Lyons, Normandy, and Luxembourg. The quartet disbanded during World War II.

In 1948 Robison wrote and recorded the comedy hit of the year, "Life Gits Tee-Jus, Don't It?" It proved to be his most popular novelty song and the most successful financially.

Cowboys and the West were favorite subjects for Robison compositions. When asked once about his talent for writing about the western scene, he replied, "Nature and tradition have always been my best sources. Whenever the dogies are rounded up, whatever chuck wagon cowboys gather round, or wherever there are camp gatherings and fiddles and guitars, there will be a tribute to that tradition."*

Modifying the music to one of the variants of the traditional cowboy song "O Bury Me Not on the Lone Prairie," Robison added music for verses, reworked the title, and composed "Carry Me Back To The Lone Prairie" in 1933. It was introduced and recorded by Metropolitan Opera star James Melton, who sang it in the Warner Brothers motion picture *Stars Over Broadway* in 1935. The song became an immediate success.

Although not a part of the parent ballad, the familiar musical strains of the verses to "Carry Me Back To The Lone Prairie" have been recorded in numerous orchestrations under the inappropriate title "Bury Me Not on the Lone Prairie."

Carson Robison never could understand why a cowboy would not want to be buried on the lone prairie. He felt that this type of rangeland was a basic part of cowboy country that had been somewhat maligned by the traditional "O Bury Me Not . . ." ballad that constantly complained about the environment. Coyotes howling, dogies wandering, and winds blowing free all had a special appeal to him.

*"Stars of the Past . . . Carson J. Robison," undated magazine clipping in Carson J. Robison file in Country Music Foundation Library, Nashville, Tennessee.

But it was not to be for Carson Robison. He was buried far from the lone prairie. In the early 1930s, he had bought a farm in Dutchess County, New York, and established his beloved CR Ranch, where he found joy and contentment in later life. He was buried in Pleasant Valley following his death on 24 March 1957.

Carson J. Robison and the Buckaroos on the roof of the Savoy Hotel in London in 1932. *Left to right:* John Mitchell, Pearl Pickens Mitchell, Carson J. Robison, Bill Mitchell. (Country Music Foundation Library and Media Center)

Carry Me Back To The Lone Prairie

Tune Ukulele
G C E A

By CARSON J. ROBISON

I'm a rov-in' cow - boy,___ far a-way from home,_____ Far___ from the
Gim-me back my sad - dle,___ gim-me back my gun,_____ Gim-me back that

prai - rie___ where I used to roam,_____ Where the dog-ies wan-der___ and the wind blows
bron - co___ that I used to run,_____ Let me spread my blank-et___ by a peace-ful

free,_____ Oh my heart is yon-der___ on the lone prai - rie.
stream,_____ Hear the cow-boys sing - in'___ by the camp-fire's gleam._____

Piano Score by
LOU LEAMAN

20 Ridin' Down That Old Texas Trail 1934

The ballad-type love song "Ridin' Down That Old Texas Trail" centers on a cowboy's vow that he will stay off the cattle trail to save a marriage commitment.

The name Texas Trail was commonly used for any early cattle trail that originated in Texas. Even the famous Chisholm Trail was labeled the Great Texas Cattle Trail on Kansas Pacific Railway maps between 1871 and 1875. Some fifty miles west, the Western Trail to Kansas and Nebraska was frequently called the Old Texas Cattle Trail. When extended to Wyoming and Montana ranges, it was also known as the Texas-Montana Trail.

Cattle trails harbored untold dangers and hardships for drovers. The northbound drives, lasting four to six months, required skill and daring on the part of the cowboy, because of the constant pushing of cattle over barren plains and mountains, fording of rivers with dangerous quicksand, exposure to violent thunderstorms that often caused the frenzy of a stampede, and the possibility of early snowstorms that could cause one delay after another. W. Baillie Grohman, English traveler and author, wrote in the *Fortnightly Review* in 1880 that in addition to these woes, "the well-known old Texas Trail" was also infested with hostile Indians and roving bands of Mexican robbers.* Little wonder that families and girlfriends were fearful about a young man hitting the trail. Also on the mind of

the girl back home might have been the concern that her lover would find other amorous interests.

The conversation between a cowboy and his girl about a possible breakup befalling them is the theme of "Ridin' Down That Old Texas Trail" by Milt Mabie and Dott Massey.

The musical Massey family was living in Midland, Texas, when New Mexico became a state in 1912. Tom, Albert, and Barney, the three oldest of seven brothers, decided to file for three sections of New Mexico rangeland in the Capitan Mountains of Lincoln County. Harsh resentment and sometimes open conflict occurred when newcomers homesteaded near existing ranches, but the Masseys were careful not to file for property near windmills or other crucial areas of established cattle operations. The Massey brothers' father moved the rest of the family into the Capitans in 1916.

A drifting cowboy from Texas worked for the Masseys in the early years in New Mexico. He refused to live indoors, preferring instead to sleep in the barn. Dott Massey and his brother-in-law Milt Mabie would go out at night and sit around an open fire, listening to the cowboy sing songs and tell stories about his experiences on the old cattle trail. Based on tales of the drifter, whose name has long been forgotten, Dott and Milt made up their song "Ridin' Down That Old Texas Trail" in 1934.

Dott Massey was born in Midland on 3 May 1910. When his two-year-old brother Allen saw the baby for the first time, he questioned, "What's dot?", and the family named the newborn Dott

---

*W. Baillie Grohman, "Cattle Ranches in the Far West," *The Fortnightly Review*, n.s., no. 1516 (1 October 1880): 438.

The Westerners. *Left to right:* Milt Mabie, Curt Massey, Louise Massey, Allen Massey, Larry Wellington. (Pecos Valley Collection, Chaves County Historical Museum, Roswell, New Mexico)

Curtis Massey. They called him by his first name, but he was to achieve musical fame as Curt Massey.

Curt Massey's father was an old-time fiddler, and he gave Curt his first lessons. Curt went on to study at the Horner Conservatory in Kansas City, Missouri. After a radio stint in Kansas City, his family moved to WLS Chicago in 1933 and soon became known as Louise Massey and the Westerners. When the group disbanded in the mid-1940s, Curt Massey worked as a single with his own shows on radio and in early television. He was musical director for two popular TV series, "The Beverly Hillbillies" and "Petticoat Junction," and he wrote the title songs for both shows.

Milton James Mabie was born in Independence, Iowa, on 27 June 1900. Because of his mother's asthma, the family moved to New Mexico when Milt was six years old. He married Louise Massey in 1916 and became an important member of the Massey family entertainment group. He died on 29 September 1973 in Roswell, New Mexico.

Ridin' Down That Old Texas Trail

By MILT MABIE
and DOTT MASSEY

Now this is the tale of the cow-boy, _____ Who dwells on that
Now list-en to me all you la-dies, _____ I've lived on that
Now I'm stay-in' home with my dar-lin' _____ I've been down that

old Tex-as trail _____ Where a man would nev-er fail, If he
old Tex-as trail _____ If a cow-boy wants to roam, You can
old Tex-as trail _____ Oh I've had a lot of fun, But my

rode down that trail, To find a pret-ty gal that he loved. _____
call him your own, If you keep him off that old Tex-as trail. _____
roam-in' days are done, And no more I'll ride that old Tex-as trail. _____

21 Ridin' Down the Canyon
1934

Smiley Burnette was the first B-class western movie sidekick to make the annual list of top ten cowboy movie stars. His comic roles and musical versatility earned him this honor for twelve consecutive years beginning in 1940.

Lester Alvin Burnette was born "with an ear for music" on 18 March 1911 in Summum, Illinois. His mother claimed there was a certain amount of rhythm in his gurgling and laughing even in early childhood. At age nine, young Burnette played a musical saw before a group of townspeople in Astoria, Illinois, and received three dollars for his performance. He organized his own band at Astoria High School and later did a one-man show in vaudeville. Burnette became proficient on fifty-two instruments from harmonica to pipe organ and could play more than a hundred in all. A pleasing personality and winning smile earned him his famous nickname.

Smiley Burnette's first radio job was on WDZ Tuscola, Illinois, the third oldest radio station in the United States. As the only employee, he served as general manager, program director, staff orchestra, chief announcer, songwriter, performer, and janitor. It was here that Smiley received a call from Gene Autry, who was then making a name for himself on WLS Chicago. Autry told Smiley he needed an accordionist and hired Smiley sight unseen.

While with "National Barn Dance" in Chicago, Gene and Smiley were discovered by Nat Levine, then head of Mascot Films, who was working

Smiley Burnette (Saturday Matinee)

on the novel idea of musical western films. He asked the two to come to Hollywood.

Autry, his wife, Ina, and Smiley left Chicago in a new Buick in the spring of 1934. While traveling through Arizona, Smiley asked Gene if he wanted to buy a song. He had previously sold many of his numbers to Autry for five dollars each. Gene asked him to sing the song, but Smiley said he hadn't written it yet. Gene replied he would pay the usual fee if the song was good. Smiley picked up a magazine lying on the back seat. The only clear space to use for writing was in a cigarette ad on the back cover. He jotted down the words as he made them up. The result was the cowboy classic "Ridin' Down the Canyon." It took Smiley three miles to finish the song. He said later he made $1.67 a mile on it.

While Gene and Smiley were working on their first feature film, *Tumbling Tumbleweeds*, in 1934, B. Reeves "Breezy" Eason, the director, overheard Smiley speaking in a froggy voice. He promptly urged Smiley to use the voice intermittently in the picture and originated the comic character "Frog Millhouse." Other familiar trademarks-to-be were a checkered shirt, a battered black hat with brim turned back, and his white horse Nellie with a black ring around her left eye. "Ridin' Down the Canyon" was featured in *Tumbling Tumbleweeds*. Gene and Smiley followed with more than fifty western films together.

In addition to appearing in the first Gene Autry western picture, Smiley Burnette also appeared in the first Roy Rogers and the first Sunset Carson productions. He was truly the "Clown Prince of Western Pictures."

Smiley was a prolific writer with more than four hundred published songs to his credit. He once wrote eleven in one day that were all used in motion pictures. In one Gene Autry film alone, eight of his songs were used.

Following his final motion picture, *Last of the Pony Riders*, in 1953, Smiley Burnette retired to concentrate on his songwriting. In 1964 he was back before the cameras in the television comedy series "Petticoat Junction." He died of leukemia on 16 February 1967 in Encino, California.

Ridin' Down the Canyon
(When the Desert Sun Goes Down)
From Tumbling Tumbleweeds

Arranged by
NICK MANOLOFF

By GENE AUTRY &
SMILEY BURNETT

Tune Uke

22 Wagon Wheels 1934

"Wagon Wheels" is an American standard. It evolved through a number of successive interpretations of one musical theme by close associates or acquaintances.

Handicapped by blindness, Hamilton Waters, a discarded slave from Maryland, was en route to Canada in a wagon with his family some time in the mid-nineteenth century. The travelers stopped for the birth of a daughter in Erie, Pennsylvania, and decided to stay. She grew up and a son was born to her in 1866. She named him Henry Thacker Burleigh, although most people would call him Harry.

When his grandfather worked as a lamplighter and town crier in Erie, young Harry made the rounds with him, leading him by the hand. The plantation songs and slave stories Harry learned from his grandfather impressed him deeply. He developed a fine voice to sing his storehouse of Negro spirituals, and in 1891 he was awarded a scholarship to study at the National Conservatory of Music in New York.

The following year Bohemian composer Antonín Dvořák (1841–1904) arrived in New York to become the director of that prestigious school. Dvořák was very impressed by traditional Negro folk songs sung for him by Harry Burleigh, by ritual music performed for his benefit in Iowa by Kickapoo Indians, and by stories of Hiawatha. Dvořák considered these indigenous American themes to be important sources on which to base musical compositions. In 1893 he finished his Symphony No. 9 in E Minor,

Opus 95 "From the New World," which made use of both Negro and American Indian music.

William Arms Fisher (1861–1948) was another student of Dvořák in New York. Commenting on the slow second-movement theme of the symphony, Fisher wrote: "The *Largo*, with its haunting English horn solo, is the outpouring of Dvořák's own home-longing, with something of the loneliness of far-off prairie horizons, the faint memory of the red-man's bygone days, and a sense of tragedy of the black man as it sings in his 'spirituals.'"*

Fisher added that the opening theme of the *Largo* gave him the lyric suggestion "Goin' home, goin' home," and he then wrote words in the Negro idiom to the rest of the melody. The result was the popular 1922 pseudo-spiritual "Goin' Home."

Another composer personally encouraged and influenced by the genius of Harry Burleigh was the popular songwriter Peter De Rose, who was born in New York's Lower East Side on 10 March 1900. While working in the stock room of a music publisher in 1920, De Rose wrote the music to his first song, "When You're Gone I Won't Forget," and sold it for $25. The success of the song led to his securing a position with the New York music publishing house of G. Ricordi & Company, where Harry Burleigh was employed as an editor.

Basing the music on "Going' Home," Peter De

*William Arms Fisher, "Anton Dvořák (1841–1904)," in "Goin' Home," from the largo of the *New World Symphony* by Anton Dvořák. Words and adaptation by William Arms Fisher [sheet music], Oliver Ditson Co., Philadelphia, 21 July 1922.

Peter De Rose (ASCAP)

Rose composed "Wagon Wheels" with Billy Hill lyrics in 1934. Even though the words clearly identify the song with the marketing and shipment of cotton, music lovers have long associated it with cowboys, and it can be found in scores of printed and recorded collections of cowboy songs.

The same songwriting team had written "There's a Home in Wyomin'" the year before. Their pioneer song, entitled "The Oregon Trail," was written in 1935, the year after "Wagon Wheels."

In addition to his songwriting, Peter De Rose performed on radio from 1923 to 1939 with May Singhi Breen, professionally known as "The Ukelele Lady." They were billed as "The Sweethearts of the Air" and were married during the sixteen-year run of the show. Probably the most famous De Rose composition was "Deep Purple," written as a piano composition in 1933. It was reintroduced as a sentimental ballad in 1939 with lyrics by Mitchell Parish. Peter De Rose died on 23 April 1953 at his New York home.

Billy Hill; his wife, the former DeDette Lee Walker; and their infant daughter, Lee De-Dette Hill, in 1933. (From *Billy Hill's American Home Songs*, Shapiro, Bernstein & Company, 1934)

WAGON WHEELS

Lyric by
BILLY HILL

Music by
PETER DE ROSE

soil I cling, I climb on my wa-gon and sing:_____

Uke in D
Capo 1st Fret
REFRAIN *Slowly and evenly*

Wa - gon Wheels, Wa - gon Wheels

p Slowly and evenly

Keep on a - turn - in' Wa - gon Wheels

Roll a - long Sing your song

23 Ole Faithful
1934

Soon after the poignant "Ole Faithful" made its appearance, it became the favorite song of Will Rogers, known and loved internationally as the American cowboy philosopher.

Rogers, who rose from a working cowboy in Oklahoma to an unofficial ambassador of good will throughout the world for American presidents, was killed in a plane crash with famed racing pilot Wiley Post on the barren wastes of Alaska near Point Barrow. "Ole Faithful" was sung at the private funeral for Rogers on 22 August 1935 in Glendale, California, by John Boles, screen actor and singing star. The familiar year-old song was thought to be a time-honored air by a *Los Angeles Times* reporter at the services who gave interrupted reflections on its rendition: "The little church . . . fragrant with flowers . . . was filled with the music of an old cowboy ballad—'Old Faithful' . . . the song of the last round-up; its echo was a sob . . . from throats toughened by the cattle dust."*

Despite its decidedly American sound, "Ole Faithful" was written in England by a Dublin-reared Jew and an Irishman. Michael Maurice Cohen, son of bookmaker and featherweight boxing champion "Cockney" Cohen, was born in Leeds, England, in 1905. He lived in Dublin as a youth but jumped a windjammer in 1924 and ended up in America. He spent some time in Hollywood, where he worked as a bit player in motion pictures and

Michael Carr (Courtesy of Ian Whitcomb)

developed an American accent. For nine months he was a cowhand in Montana, and he later played the piano in a Las Vegas gambling joint called the Golden Bar. In 1929 he returned to England and became a songwriter.

Michael Cohen changed his last name to Carr in 1933 and began composing songs for music hall artists including English comedienne Gracie Fields. Some of his most popular works were Irish songs. Carr collaborated with the Kennedy brothers, Hamilton and Jimmy, to produce popular songs, London Palladium scores, and film musi-

*"Stars, Dignitaries and Range Riders Weep at Last Rites for Will Rogers," *Los Angeles Times*, 23 August 1935.

J. Hamilton Kennedy, Irish
songwriter, in October 1949.
(BBC Enterprises)

cals. Carr and Hamilton Kennedy wrote "Ole Faithful" in 1934.

Joseph Hamilton Kennedy was born in Tyrone, Northern Ireland, in 1908. He was a graduate of Dublin University and became a schoolmaster. In the 1930s Kennedy began writing songs while traveling around England, Canada, and the United States. When he returned to England, he teamed up with Carr on a number of cowboy songs.

Kennedy joined the British Broadcasting Corporation in 1940 as an announcer and producer. His most famous program was "Folk's Choice," later to be called "Housewife's Choice." Other radio programs were "Call of the West" and "Stars For a Night." He died in London on 1 April 1954.

Gene Autry sang "Ole Faithful" to his horse Champion in his 1936 Republic feature *The Big Show*. Roy Rogers sang it to his horse ten years later in the Republic picture *My Pal Trigger*.

Old Faithful was an affectionate name earned only by dependable cow horses during the old days. Adolph Huffmeyer had a South Texas cow horse that was already named Old Faithful when he bought it. The animal lived up to its name more than once.

Huffmeyer worked as a cowboy in Frio County. In the fall of 1878 he left for Old Mexico to buy cattle. Needing the best horse he could find for a month of steady work, the cowboy paid $75 for Old Faithful, three times more than ordinary cow horses were bringing. As Huffmeyer neared his destination outside Agua Sola bandits tried to overtake him, but his new mount outdistanced them. After buying his cattle, he hired four vaqueros to help drive the steers back to Texas.

During the first night north of the Rio Grande, the cattle stampeded at 3:00 A.M. when a goat snorted at a nearby ranch. Again, the reliable horse proved its worth. Huffmeyer wrote: "After running several hundred yards Old Faithful and I got in ahead of the cattle and checked their mad rush, and as soon as the vaqueros came up we rounded them up and held them until daylight."*

*A. Huffmeyer, "Buying Longhorns in Old Mexico," *Frontier Times* 13, no. 3 (December 1935): 147.

Ole Faithful

By MICHAEL CARR
and HAMILTON KENNEDY

Ole Faith-ful, we rode the range to-ge-ther Ole Faith-ful, in ev-'ry kind of weather, When your round-up days are ov-er There'll be pastures white with clo-ver, For you, Ole Faith-ful, pal o' mine._____ Hur-ry

24 Cowboy's Heaven
1934

After living eighteen months with the wild riders of the plains, a writer from back east attempted to dispel the generally held opinion that all cowboys were irreligious and ungodly. He wrote in *Lippincott's Magazine* in 1881 that gun-belted Texas cowhands, seated in a crude brush arbor, listened reverently to one of their own read the Scriptures and were captivated when the danger of going astray was explained to them with typical cowboy brevity: "If you lose your property, you may acquire more; if you lose your wife, you may marry again; if you lose your children, you may have more; but if you lose your immortal soul, then up the spout you go."[*]

A common belief held by old-time range riders was that God himself had been a cowboy before becoming the Range Boss in the sky and that heaven was the "home corral," a perpetually green cattle country, well-watered, never overstocked, safe from storms, and permanently inhabited by the favorite horse of the deceased. When a partner of Captain Eugene B. Millett died in the late 1860s, the pioneer Texas and Kansas cattleman expressed hope that, when his friend stood in final judgment, "the Great Herder" would tell him, "You have been inspected and branded, enter in, for you have done many good deeds on the way."[†]

Frankie Marvin wrote a song in 1934 about a cowboy's vision of the "great beyond" and of sharing the ranges on the other shore with his best mount. He titled it "Cowboy's Heaven."

Frank James Marvin, of Frankie and Johnny Marvin radio, recording, and songwriting fame, was born on 27 January 1904 in Butler, Oklahoma.

Frankie Marvin

[*]Louis C. Bradford, "Among the Cowboys," *Lippincott's Magazine*, n.s. 1, no. 6 (June 1881): 565.
[†]"Pioneer of the West," *Ellsworth* (Kansas) *Messenger*, 10 February 1916.

When Frankie was only five or six years old, his brother Johnny left home to travel with a circus, eventually ending up in New York City writing "down home" songs, appearing in his own daily radio show nationwide on NBC, and making phonograph records.

When Johnny Marvin returned home for a visit, his young brother Frankie had learned every one of his songs from listening to records. Frankie returned to New York with Johnny and in six months had his own record contract.

In the late 1920s Frankie Marvin appeared with Whitey Ford, the "Duke of Paducah," in a comedy duo known as Ralph and Elmer. He met singing cowboy Gene Autry in New York in 1929, beginning a lifelong friendship and a twenty-five year professional association. Autry moved to Chicago in the early 1930s and on to Hollywood in 1934. Frankie Marvin joined Autry in California to begin a musical career with his friend in personal appearances, radio, movies, and eventually on television. His steel guitar style was a distinctive part of the Gene Autry sound.

"Cowboy's Heaven" was patterned on the style and structure of cowboy ballads. Gene Autry helped with revisions after Frankie sold it to him for $50. In 1934 the song appeared in sheet music as well as in the song folio *"The Oklahoma Cowboy" Gene Autry's Famous Cowboy Songs and Mountain Ballads*. Both issues were published by the M. M. Cole Publishing Company of Chicago.

Cowboys have always been noted for saying a lot in few words. In his foreword to the 1933 Jules Verne Allen book *Cowboy Lore*, William Thomas Carley of Victoria, Texas, was typically concise when he described the eternal home of the cowboy as a place "where there's plenty of fat cattle, no sheep, no alkali, no dry water holes, no 'chip-carts,' but plenty of wood and good horses—Cowboy Heaven."*

*Jules Verne Allen, *Cowboy Lore* (San Antonio: The Naylor Co., 1933), vii.

Cowboy's Heaven

Arranged by
NICK MANOLOFF

By GENE AUTRY &
FRANKIE MARVIN

Tune Uke

A D F# B

25 I Want To Be A Cowboy's Sweetheart! 1934

Ruby Blevins was the only girl in a family of eleven children. She was born on 30 October 1912 near Hot Springs, Arkansas. After teaching herself to play the guitar and taking violin lessons, she got her first music job at the age of fourteen. Ruby added the letter *e* to her first name to get the "homespun" out of it and moved to California in 1928. She became enchanted with cowboy and western music and landed a job on KMTR Hollywood as "Rubye Blevins, the Yodeling Cowgirl from San Antone."

In 1930 Rubye joined a band of entertainers assembled by Stuart Hamblen for a regular radio show on KMIC Inglewood. Two other girls, Lorraine McIntire and Ruthy DeMondrum, were members of the group. Hamblen saw that radio audiences might have a problem distinguishing between the names Ruthy and Rubye on the air, so Rubye changed her first name to Patsy and later added Montana. The three girls were billed as the Montana Cowgirls.

Patsy went back home to Arkansas in 1933 for a visit, where her brothers Clyde and Ken had decided to enter what they called "the world's biggest watermelon" in the Chicago World's Fair. Patsy went along and while there heard that the Kentucky Ramblers of WLS "National Barn Dance" fame were seeking a female vocalist. She tried out and was hired. Because of her western image and the growing popularity of cowboy songs, the group renamed themselves the Prairie Ramblers.

The first song Patsy sang on WLS was "Montana

Patsy Montana

Plains," written as "Texas Plains" by her former associate Stuart Hamblen back in California. Hamblen was not pleased with her changing the title and setting, so Patsy decided to write her own musical trademark in a similar structure and rhythm. The result was "I Want To Be A Cowboy's Sweetheart!"

Weekdays, between WLS broadcasts, Patsy was busy on the road with a live show called the "Round-Up of WLS Radio Stars," featuring Gene

Autry, Smiley Burnette, Max Terhune, Pat Buttram, and others. While with the touring group, she fell in love with and married Paul E. Rose, manager of the Mac and Bob act. In 1934, during performances in Illinois, Rose was away for several days visiting his sick mother in Knoxville, Tennessee. Lonely in her hotel room one evening, she wrote "I Want To Be A Cowboy's Sweetheart!" The title had been suggested earlier by country-music promoter J. L. Frank. Patsy introduced the song on "National Barn Dance," and it became her lifetime trademark.

Patsy later sang her song on WOR radio in New York City, and music publisher Bob Miller arranged an audition with Art Satherly of the American Record Company. She recorded "I Want To Be A Cowboy's Sweetheart!" in August 1935. It became her biggest hit, and of the more than two hundred published and recorded songs written by Patsy Montana, it is the one that has survived throughout the years. It helped her become the first female country and western singer to sell a million records.

Patsy Montana met thousands of cowboys. Frequently one would tell her that "I Want To Be A Cowboy's Sweetheart!" was written for him alone and that every time she sang it she must have had him in mind. In time it became her tribute to all her cowboy sweethearts, those in heaven as well as those still riding the range.

I Want To Be A Cowboy's Sweetheart !

Words and Music by
PATSY MONTANA

26 The Cattle Call
1934

Reliable evidence even suggesting the yodel was part of old-time cowboy songs is rare. Jack Thorpe, who collected authentic cowboy songs and published the first collection, did not even address the subject in his writings. One researcher has made the following conclusion: "It is tempting, and probably defensible, to theorize that the traditional cowboy yodel, if such a thing ever reached the status of music, was a falsetto melodic device like what Eddy Arnold used in 'Cattle Call,' rather than a conventional yodel." *

True cattle calls were improvised yells, shouts, or hollers, used on the open range by cowboys to help in their work with cows. Each cowboy developed individual calls according to his own vocalization limits and the need or mood of the moment. Starting a herd, driving cattle, and penning them all required different types of calls. A quasi-musical melody helped to control the restlessness of drifting, milling, and bedding cattle.

Falsetto yells appear to have been uncommon on the range but no doubt were used by some cowboys. They were not the yodeling styles developed by movie cowboys of the 1930s, which reintroduced some Swiss elements, but rather a high-pitched "ee-yow," "hi-yi," "yippee," or similar call that found its way into an occasional cowboy ballad.

*Robert Coltman, "Roots of the Country Yodel: Notes Toward a Life History," *John Edwards Memorial Foundation Quarterly* 12, no. 42 (Summer 1976): 91.

Doie Hensley Owens, better known as Tex Owens, wrote "The Cattle Call" in 1934. Like Eddy Arnold he made an octave leap into a cattle-soothing "woo-hoo, woo-hoo hoo hoo" when performing his own composition, but without a yodel break in his voice.

Tex Owens was born in Bell County, Texas, on 15 June 1892. He had ten sisters and one brother. His sister Ruby became the popular cowgirl singer Texas Ruby, who later married perennial champion fiddler Curley Fox.

At age fifteen, Tex went to work on a ranch but soon joined the Cordell Wagon Show after a performance of the troupe not far from the ranch. After a stint with the show, Tex traveled around Texas, Oklahoma, and Kansas. At one time he was a working cowboy on the King Ranch. While with a construction crew working on a bridge near Paola, Kansas, in 1916, he met and married Maude Neal. They had two daughters, Laura Lee and Dolpha Jane.

Tex Owens started in radio in 1928 and became a regular entertainer on KMBC Kansas City, Missouri, in 1931. While he was waiting to do a broadcast from the eleventh floor studios in the Pickwick Hotel one day in 1934, snow began to fall. Looking out the window, Tex began to feel sorry for all the hungry livestock out in the open that were trying to survive the frigid weather. His thoughts turned to calling cattle in to feed as he had done back on the ranch as a young man. In thirty minutes Tex wrote

Tex Owens (Courtesy of Maude J. Owens)

"The Cattle Call" to a melody remindful of "The Morning Star Waltz."

Laura Lee and Dolpha Jane joined their father as singers on the Brush Creek Follies over KMBC in 1936 as Joy and Jane. Laura Lee went on to become the first female singer with Bob Wills and His Texas Playboys and was billed as "The Queen of Western Swing." In 1939 Tex left Kansas City and moved to Cleveland, Ohio, where he broadcasted over WTAM. He appeared later at WLW Cincinnati on the Boone County Jamboree.

Tex Owens went to California in the mid-1940s for radio work and roles in two motion pictures. In 1948 he landed a part in the John Wayne cattle epic *Red River*. Ten days and thirty-five experienced horsemen were required to film the panic of a cattle stampede on location in southern Arizona. Tex suffered a broken back and fractured arm when his horse fell with him during the shooting. He was confined to a hospital in Nogales for a year

of treatment and recuperation, returning to radio in 1950 at KOAM Pittsburg, Kansas. Ten years later, he moved to New Baden, Texas, and died unexpectedly at his Camp Creek home on 9 September 1962.

The Cattle Call

Words and Music by
TEX OWENS

27 Allá en el Rancho Grande 1934

Conflict exists concerning the authorship of "Allá en el Rancho Grande" because it entered the public domain in Mexico through lack of copyright registration within a specified time. At that time Mexican law provided that copyrights were in effect only during the period spent in publication plus one additional year.

Records of the Instituto Nacional de Bellas Artes

in Mexico City show that the song was written in 1918 by Guzman Aguilera, author of the words, and Lorenzo Barcelata, composer of the music.

An uncopyrighted version of the song, published in Mexico in 1926, gives credit to Silvano R. Ramos for the composition. The following March his music was revised by Lopez Alaves and published in a copyrighted edition by Salvador Cabrera of Mexico City.

Also in 1927, "Allá en el Rancho Grande" was published by A. Wagner and Levien of Mexico City, with words by J. D. del Moral and music arranged by Emilio D. Uranga. Although the composition bears a notice of copyright, no record of registration has been located. The music of this composition is identical to that of the one copyrighted earlier in the year by Salvador Cabrera, although the lyrics are different.

Meanwhile the song was being passed along orally by vaqueros and cowboys in Texas. In 1930 the Texas Folk-Lore Society printed "El Rancho Grande" in an article with the same Spanish lyrics used in later popular American editions. Also printed was a literal translation of the Spanish words that had become a part of the repertory of cowboys on Texas ranches:

Down there at the big ranch,
Down there where I lived,
There was a little ranch maid
Who gaily said to me:

"I am going to make you some trousers
Like those worn by the ranchmen.
I shall begin them with wool
But will finish them in leather."

The greatest joy of the ranchman
Is to have a good horse,
To saddle him in the afternoon
And go out to see the stock.*

On 26 March 1934, the Edward B. Marks Music Corporation of New York copyrighted "Allá en el Rancho Grande." In their first printing of the song, acknowledgment was given to J. del Moral for the Spanish lyrics, Bartley Costello for new English lyrics, and Emilio D. Uranga for the music. A later edition by the same company lauded the enormous Decca hit record by Bing Crosby but changed the credit for both Spanish lyrics and music to the earlier writer, Silvano R. Ramos.

Bartley C. (Bart) Costello, contributor of the popularized American lyrics to "Allá en el Rancho Grande" that have become standard, was a Tin Pan Alley songwriter. A native of Rutland, Vermont, he was born on 21 January 1871. In addition to writing songs, Costello was active in the publishing business in New York. He died on 14 January 1941.

A different version of the Mexican cowboy song came out in 1939 when Stasny Music Corporation of New York published "I Have a Rancho Grande (Allá en el Rancho Grande)." The Spanish form of this less popular version was credited to J. del Moral and Paul Barragan with re-created English words by Al Jacobs. The music was ascribed to Emilio d'Uranga and Al Jacobs. This version was successfully introduced on the NBC Radio network by Los Rancheros, Mexico's outstanding ambassadors of song.

At different times, Al T. Jacobs (Mercedes

Snapshot, *left to right*, Bartley C. "Bart" Costello, his sister Jane, and his brother John in Atlantic City, New Jersey, in 1913. (Courtesy of Walter A. Costello)

Gabril) was in managerial positions with a number of music publishing houses. He was born in San Francisco, California, on 22 January 1903 and became successful as a radio pianist, singer, and songwriter for motion pictures.

*Jovita Gonzáles, "Tales and Songs of the Texas-Mexicans," *Publications of the Texas Folk-Lore Society* 8 (1930): 86.

ALLÁ EN EL RANCHO GRANDE
My Ranch

English Lyrics by
BARTLEY COSTELLO

Spanish Lyric by
J. del MORAL

Tune Uke

G C E A

Music by
EMILIO D. URANGA

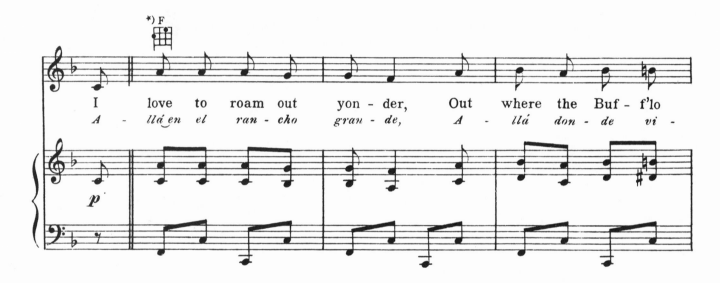

*) Symbols are for Banjo or Guitar

rop - ing and a - ty - ing, I'm rop - ing and a - ty - ing.____
*le - gre me de - cí - a, Que a le - gre me de - cí - a.*____

VERSE

Give me my ranch and my cat - tle,____
Give me my bri - dle and sad - dle,____
Te voy ha - cer tus cal - zo - nes,

____ Far from the great cit - y's rat - tle;____
____ And my old Pin - to I'll strad - dle;____
____ *Co - mo los u - sa el ran - che - ro;*

Give me a big herd to bat - tle, _____ For I just
I'll get the cow - boys a - rid - ing, _____ Out where the
Te los co - mien - - zo de la - na, _____ *Te los a -*

C7

love herd - ing cat - tle.
rust - - lers are hi - ding.
ca - - bo de cue - ro.

F

D.S.

Fine

D.S.

varias veces

3rd Verse

Some-times the winter storms tearing,
Set all the cattle a-raring,
But when the winter is over,
We're sure enough in the clover.

Nunca te fies de promesas
Ni mucho menos de amores
Que si te dan calabzas
Verás lo que son ardores.

4th Verse

Give me the wide open spaces,
That's just where I know my place is,
I love the Ro-de-o dearly,
And the Big Round-Up yearly.

Pon muy atento el oído
Cuando rechine la puerta
Hay muertos que no hacen ruido
Y son muy gordas sus penas.

5th Verse

Tho' we play seven eleven,
My Ranch is next door to Heaven,
We smile when we take a beatin',
But hang a rat when he's cheatin'.

Cuando te pidan cigarro
No des cigarro y cerillo
Porque si das las dos cosas
Te tantearán de zorrillo.

28 Take Me Back To My Boots And Saddle   1935

One of the classic songs about the cattle country, "Take Me Back To My Boots And Saddle" was envisioned and partly written in the rooftop garden of a downtown New York hotel.

On a beautiful summer day in 1935, Walter Samuels was courting his wife-to-be, Ruth Altschul, who lived in the Hotel Olcott on Seventy-second Street in New York City. While they were seated in the penthouse garden, the idea of a cowboy song came to him and he wrote part of it while on the rooftop. Samuels took the unfinished song to his close friends Teddy Powell and Lenny Whitcup for their contributions. Once the song was finished, all three felt they had a hit. When they took the song down to Tin Pan Alley the next day, however, nobody seemed to want it. All the music publishers they contacted turned it down.

By 5 o'clock that afternoon the tired threesome

Walter G. Samuels

Leonard Whitcup (Courtesy of Sally Whitcup)

had just about given up. On the way to the subway, they happened to think of another publisher they knew and decided to give it one more try. Luckily, Bob Miller of Schuster & Miller was still in. The three told Miller they had a beautiful western song, and he agreed to hear it. Samuels played "Take Me Back To My Boots And Saddle" on the piano, and Miller accepted it on the spot. In a few weeks, ten different recordings of the song had been made.

The three successful composers had met a number of years before in the Catskill Mountains. Samuels was head counselor and social activities chairman at the adult-oriented Grossinger Camp where he met Powell and Whitcup. Their musical backgrounds and songwriting interests turned a chance meeting into a longtime professional association and close friendship.

Walter Gerald Samuels was born in New York City on 2 February 1908. He studied piano for fifteen years before becoming a composer and entertainer. He was in the South Pacific with the army during World War II and wrote twenty-five battalion songs. Samuels studied law at New York Uni-

versity, but he became a composer, author, and publisher of popular music. In time he wrote the musical scores for twenty Gene Autry and Roy Rogers motion pictures.

Teddy Raymond Powell, professional name for Alfred Paoella, was a westerner by birth, having been born in Oakland, California, on 1 March 1906. He was with the Abe Lyman Orchestra for seventeen years as a violinist and guitarist before embarking on a career as a bandleader late in 1939. His orchestra made its debut at the New York nightclub Famous Door and appeared throughout the United States in hotels, nightclubs, theaters, and films from 1940 until 1946, when the band folded. Years later Powell formed the Tee Pee Music Company in New York City.

Leonard Whitcup, composer, lyricist, and publisher, was also a native of New York City and an alumnus of New York University. He was born on 12 October 1903 and in early life became associated with summer camps in New Hampshire as both a counselor for boys and a producer of variety shows. Whitcup became very active in New York writing his own songs and scores for radio, vaudeville, and Broadway revues. His song, "Shout Wherever You May Be, I Am an American," was cited in the *Congressional Record* on 5 May 1941 for the beauty of its lyrics and the power of its music. Whitcup died on 6 April 1979.

In addition to "Take Me Back To My Boots And Saddle," Samuels, Powell, and Whitcup collaborated on such song successes as "I Couldn't Believe My Eyes," "March Winds and April Showers," "Heaven Help This Heart of Mine," and "If My Heart Could Only Talk."

"Take Me Back To My Boots And Saddle" became one of the most popular cowboy songs ever written. On 16 November 1935, it made its first appearance on "Your Hit Parade" and ran for eleven consecutive weeks.

Take Me Back To My
Boots And Saddle

Words and Music by
WALTER G. SAMUELS
LEONARD WHITCUP
TEDDY POWELL

Take Me Back To My Boots And Saddle

29 Don't Fence Me In
1935

Robert Henry Fletcher was born in Clear Lake, Iowa, on 13 March 1885 and moved to Montana with his parents at an early age. His father's cattle were wiped out on the lower Yellowstone ranges during the disastrous 1886–87 winter of prolonged blizzards and sub-zero temperatures. His firsthand knowledge of life on the northern ranges and his personal contact with pioneers gave authority to Bob Fletcher's numerous stories, poems, and songs about the Montana cattle industry. A book of his poetry and prose was published in 1934 under the title *Corral Dust*.

In the fall of 1935, Hollywood movie producer Lou Brock commissioned Bob Fletcher to assist in writing authentic western dialogue for a musical film extravaganza to be entitled *Adios Argentina*. Cole Porter was hired to do the music. Prior to departing for Hollywood, Fletcher composed several songs and took them along. His original lyrics and melody to one he called "Don't Fence Me In" contained three verses and the following chorus:

> Don't fence me in,
> Give me land, lots of land
> Stretching miles across the West,
> Don't fence me in,
> Let me ride where it's wide
> For somehow I like it best,
> I want to see the stars, I want to feel the
>   breeze,

I want to smell the sage and hear the
   cottonwood trees,
Just turn me loose,
Let me straddle my old saddle
Where the Rocky Mountains rise,
On my cayuse
I'll go sifting, I'll go drifting

Cole Porter (ASCAP)

140

Robert H. Fletcher (Courtesy of Robert K. Fletcher and Virginia F. MacDonald)

Underneath those western skies.
I've got to get where the West commences
I can't stand hobbles, I can't stand fences,
Don't fence me in!*

In Hollywood, Bob Fletcher showed Cole Porter the songs. For some reason, Twentieth Century-Fox never produced the film. After Fletcher returned to Montana, Porter offered to buy "Don't Fence Me In" for $250. Fletcher accepted with the stipulation that if the song were ever published he would receive some sort of recognition. Porter rewrote the music and two verses and altered the words to the chorus.

In 1944 Warner Brothers acquired "Don't Fence Me In," and cowboy star Roy Rogers introduced it in the star-studded wartime musical *Hollywood Canteen*. He sang it again the following year in his own Republic motion picture *Don't Fence Me In*.

"Don't Fence Me In" made its own contribution to national morale during World War II with what Americans considered an appropriate statement to

*C. J. Doherty, "Montana Objects," *Missoula County* (Mont.) *Times*, 13 November 1945.

Adolph Hitler from a free country. In live radio broadcasts, Kate Smith made the song a major hit and eulogized Cole Porter as the composer of the song. Recordings by Roy Rogers, Kate Smith, Bing Crosby, and the Andrews Sisters sold millions of discs, and for eight weeks the song was number 1 on "Your Hit Parade."

Meanwhile, newscaster Walter Winchell broke the story that Porter had bought the song from a Montana cowboy named Fletcher. Twenty years after the song appeared Bob Fletcher was finally recognized as the original composer of "Don't Fence Me In." With the assistance of the American Society of Composers, Authors, and Publishers, he was able to work out a modest royalty agreement with representatives of Cole Porter, who was then seriously ill.

In 1960 Bob Fletcher wrote *Free Grass to Fences*, a definitive book about the Montana cattle ranges. He died on 20 November 1972 in San Diego, California.

Cole Albert Porter was one of the greatest American composers of popular music, writing many successful musical comedies and music for motion pictures. His songs include "Begin the Beguine," "Night and Day," "So In Love Am I," and "What Is This Thing Called Love?" He was born in Peru, Indiana, on 9 June 1891, and died in Santa Monica, California, on 15 October 1964.

DON'T FENCE ME IN

From the Warner Bros. Picture
"HOLLYWOOD CANTEEN"

Words and Music by
COLE PORTER
A.S.C.A.P.

142   Don't Fence Me In

30 The Hills Of Old Wyomin' 1936

One of the most popular songs ever written about Wyoming was composed in Palm Springs, California, by two songwriters who had never been there.

The Hollywood songwriting team of Leo Robin and Ralph Rainger wrote "The Hills Of Old Wyomin'" in 1936, at a time when they were writing songs for as many as a dozen musical films a year for Paramount Pictures. Love was a favorite topic with them and "I love you" was invariably their lyric theme. Robin had once written advice to the lovelorn in a lonely hearts newspaper column, and many of his lyrics had their source in the letters he received.

Ralph Rainger (ASCAP)

Leo Robin (ASCAP)

144

CHEYENNE

(SHY ANN)

SONG

WORDS BY
HARRY WILLIAMS
MUSIC BY
EGBERT VAN ALSTYNE

5

JEROME H. REMICK & CO.
successors to the
WHITNEY-WARNER PUB. CO.
NEW YORK   DETROIT

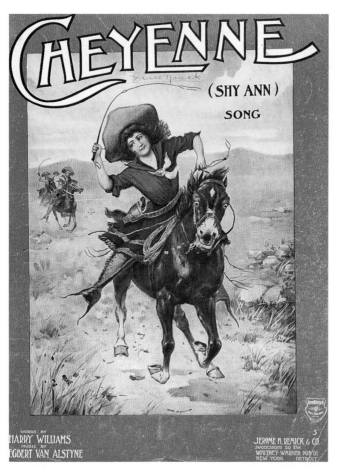

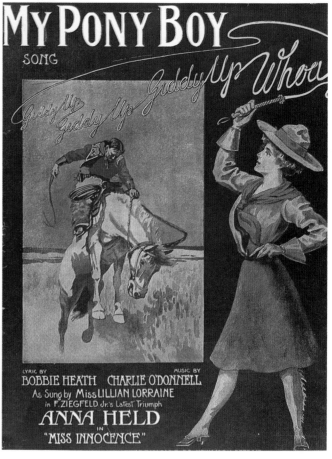

WHEN IT'S SPRINGTIME
IN THE ROCKIES
Charming Waltz Song

WITH
UKELELE
ARRANGEMENT

Words and Music by
MARY HALE WOOLSEY
ROBERT SAUER
MILT TAGGART

Featured by
"COUSIN" PAUL CRUTCHFIELD
"The Georgia Cracker" K. M. A. Shenendoah, Ia.

Villa Moret

MEXICALI ROSE
WALTZ BALLAD
WORDS BY
HELEN STONE
MUSIC BY
JACK B. TENNEY

SUCCESSFULLY FEATURED BY
CYRIL GODWIN
and his CAPITOL THEATRE ORCHESTRA
Calgary, Canada

Published by
W. A. Quincke & Co.
Los Angeles, Calif.

THE UTAH TRAIL
(SECOND EDITION)

As Sung and Introduced by
"BOB AND MONTE"

Words and Music by
"BOB" PALMER

ROBERT PALMER
PUBLISHING CO.
Los Angeles, Calif.

The NEW
CARSON ROBISON
SONG ALBUM

WITH GUITAR
AND UKELELE
CHORDS

2ND
EDITION

NBC

22
COMPLETE SONGS
including
"BARNACLE BILL
THE SAILOR"
"LEFT MY GAL IN
THE MOUNTAINS"
"GOIN' BACK TO TEXAS"
"IN THE CUMBERLAND
MOUNTAINS"

CARSON ROBISON AND HIS PIONEERS

SOUTHERN MUSIC PUB CO Inc
1619 BROADWAY NEW YORK

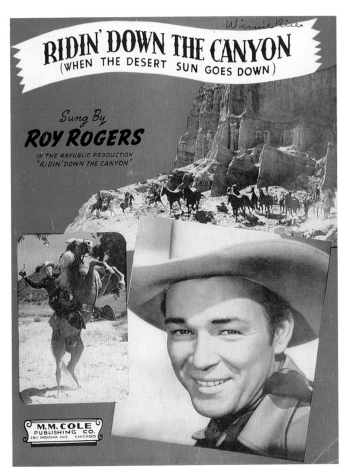

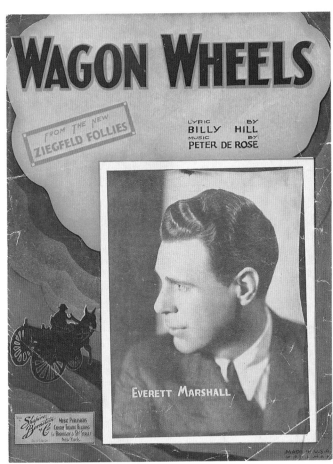

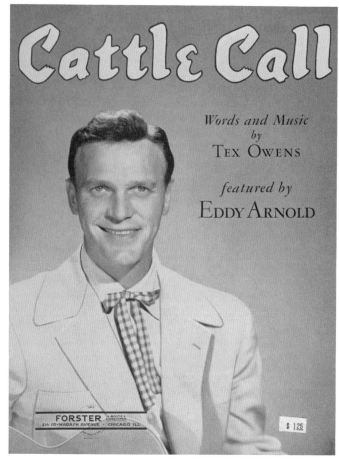

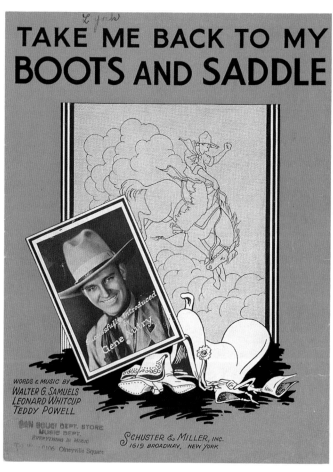

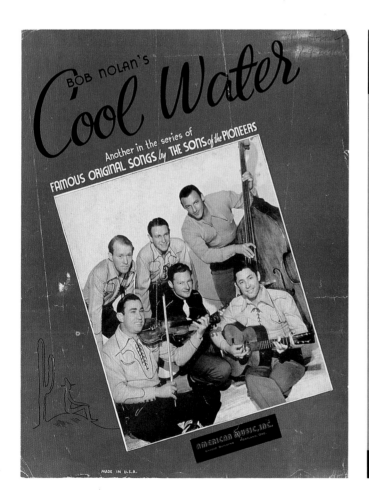

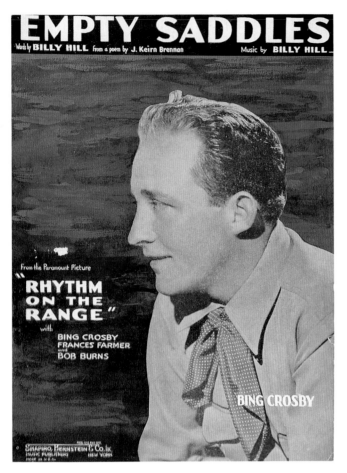

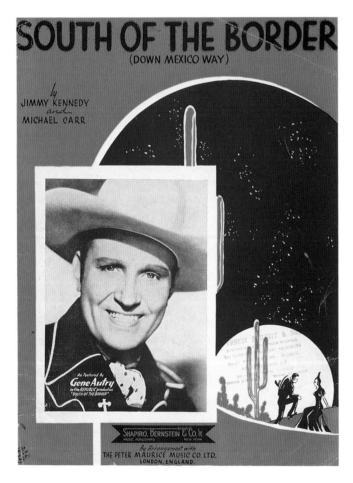

The Everlasting Hills Of Oklahoma

Words and Music by TIM SPENCER

Successfully Recorded by
SONS OF THE PIONEERS
for Victor Records

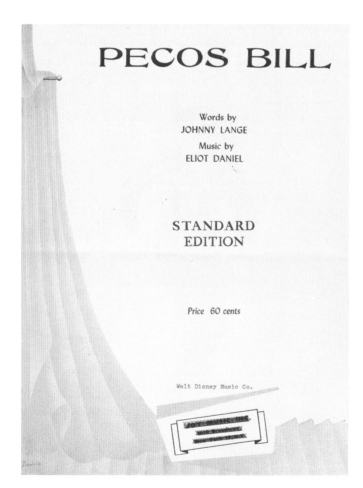

TIM SPENCER MUSIC, INC.
Sole Selling Agents
HILL and RANGE SONGS, INC
7164 Melrose Avenue
Hollywood 46, Calif.

BLUE SHADOWS ON THE TRAIL

Words: Johnny Lange   Music: Eliot Daniel

WALT DISNEY'S
NEW HIT MUSICAL

"Melody Time"

BLUE SHADOWS ON THE TRAIL
MELODY TIME
PECOS BILL
LITTLE TOOT
APPLE SONG
THE PIONEER SONG
THE LORD IS GOOD TO ME

SANTLY-JOY, INC.
Music Publishers
New York 19, N. Y.

PECOS BILL

Words by
JOHNNY LANGE

Music by
ELIOT DANIEL

STANDARD
EDITION

Price 60 cents

Walt Disney Music Co.

RIDERS IN THE SKY
A Cowboy Legend

Words and Music by
STAN JONES

AS ORIGINALLY INTRODUCED
BY *Burl Ives*

EDWIN H. MORRIS & COMPANY, INC.
1619 Broadway   New York, N. Y.

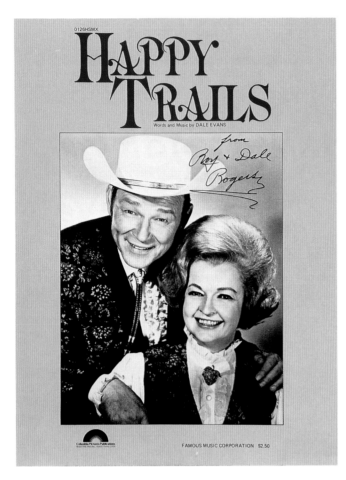

Asked to write the musical interludes for a motion picture, Robin and Rainger had to compose songs that fit particular film situations, were free of anachronisms, and were within the range of the intended singer.

The two experts went about their work in a logical manner. They studied the range of the singer and the limits of the picture and suited the tempo for the scene. They made sure that certain vowels did not land on the high notes and certain consonants on the low ones. Rainger first wrote the melody for a melody singer like Bing Crosby. Robin first wrote the words for a lyric singer like Maurice Chevalier. Given seven notes and the intervening halftones for the melodies, Robin and Rainger became one of the foremost songwriting teams in Hollywood and wrote one romantic hit after another.

"The Hills Of Old Wyomin'" was written for the 1936 Paramount picture *Palm Springs*, starring Frances Langford and Smith Ballew. Cowboy star Eddie Dean also sang the song in his Producers Releasing Corporation film *Song of Old Wyoming* in 1945, co-starring Jennifer Holt.

Robin and Rainger visited Wyoming for the first time in late 1936. There they received the plaudits of civic groups throughout the state, and Governor Leslie A. Miller gave special thanks to the composers for capturing the true spirit of Wyoming in song.

Lyric writer Leo Robin was born on 6 April 1895, in Pittsburgh, Pennsylvania, and studied law at the University of Pittsburgh.

Ralph Rainger was born Ralph Reichenthal in New York City on 7 October 1901. He attended Brown University, New Jersey Law School, and the Walter Damrosch Institute of Musical Art.

Despite their training in law, Robin and Rainger had their hearts set on careers in music. Robin broke into songwriting in 1925 when his work was included in the Broadway production *By the Way.* He collaborated with Clifford Grey in 1927 to write "Hallelujah!" for *Hit the Deck*. Rainger became interested in music in high school and became an accomplished pianist. He was featured with Edgar

"Cookie" Fairchild as a piano duo in the Broadway musical *Queen High* in 1927 and in the *Ziegfeld Follies of 1927.* In 1929 Rainger and Adam Carroll played as a double piano team in *The Little Show.* His first composition, "Moanin' Low," was featured in that show.

Leo Robin went to Hollywood in 1928, when he was signed by Paramount Pictures as a lyric writer for the 1929 Maurice Chevalier motion picture *Innocents in Paris*. The next year he wrote songs for *Monte Carlo*, in which Jeanette MacDonald introduced "Beyond the Blue Horizon."

Ralph Rainger arrived in Hollywood in 1931. He and Robin were a songwriting team with Paramount from 1932 until 1938, when they moved to Twentieth Century–Fox. Death separated the team in 1942, when Ralph Rainger was killed in a plane crash on 23 October near Palm Springs, California. Leo Robin died on 29 December 1984 in the Motion Picture and Television Hospital in suburban Los Angeles.

Featured in the Paramount Picture "Palm Springs"

The Hills Of Old Wyomin'

Words and Music by
LEO ROBIN &
RALPH RAINGER

Molto Moderato (*leisurely*)

★ *Symbols for Guitar*

Wake with a song! Wake with the sun!

Sad-dle to mend, cat - tle to tend, Plen - ty to be

done._____ Let me live_____ on the range_____

Where a man has room to roam in_____ And

31 Cool Water 1936

Soon after composing "Tumbling Leaves" in 1932 and following a short leave from the Rocky Mountaineers, Bob Nolan was recruited a second time to help form another western trio by Leonard Slye, who was soon to achieve movie stardom as Roy Rogers. In the meantime, Missouri-born Vernon "Tim" Spencer had filled the vacancy left by

Bob Nolan (Saturday Matinee)

Nolan, and the group had gone through two more name changes, the International Cowboys and the O Bar O Cowboys. Slye, Nolan, and Spencer formed the Pioneers Trio in late 1933, auditioned at KFWB in Los Angeles, and began a daily radio program. Hugh Farr of Texas, one of the premier fiddlers of all time, joined them in 1934 and added his mellow bass voice to the close harmony of the trio. Whether by chance or design, KFWB announcer Harry Hall commented on the air one day in March 1934 that the singers were too young to be actual pioneers but that they certainly were "sons of the pioneers." The trio liked that. This new name and their impeccable harmony prompted cowboy movie comic Gabby Hayes to comment, "That Pioneer family shore raised a bunch of good singers."

The Bob Nolan composition "Tumbling Leaves" underwent a name change to "Tumbling Tumbleweeds" and became the theme song of the Sons of the Pioneers on their daily one-hour radio show.

The Sons of the Pioneers began a series of Standard Transcriptions for radio, and in 1934 they made their first records for the Decca Recording Company. The first movie for the young quartet was *The Old Homestead*, released in 1935 by Liberty Pictures. The following year, the outstanding guitar playing of Karl Farr, youngest brother of Hugh Farr, added further music versatility to their sound. Then began a string of movies unparalleled by any other cowboy musical group. This initial organization became the foremost of all western sing-

ing performers. But even with fame and success, the spell of the desert and its power of the mirage was forever in the soul of Bob Nolan. In it he found beauty and solace.

The beauty and cruelty of the silent Arizona wastelands made a decided impact on Bob Nolan in his youth, and it drew him back time and again. While still a student at Tucson High School (1924–27), Nolan wrote a poem entitled "Cool Water," a commentary on the ceaseless conflict between truth and illusion. From that poem came the heartrending musical image of a desert traveler almost delirious from lack of water and the disappearance of shimmering water holes. Racked with pain and thirst, the man and his sore-footed horse ultimately yearn more for death than for the cool water that seems to evaporate into a merciless expanse of sand before their eyes.

In a national survey conducted in 1951, "Cool Water" was found to be "the best-known song of the American West."

In 1979 the Smithsonian Institution honored the Sons of the Pioneers as a national treasure, and Bob Nolan, who had been called "the finest songwriter ever to appear in country music," was credited with inventing the sound and style of western harmony singing.

Six days before his death, Bob Nolan granted a rare taped interview to Bill Bowen of *Pioneer*

A tantalizing mirage, shimmering in the distance, beckons thirst-racked travelers. In the words of songwriter Bob Nolan, the deceptive illusion is work of a devil who "spreads the burning sand with water." (Emil Schulthess for Black Star)

News. During the session, Nolan recited a lengthy poem, one of many stored only in his productive mind. He called it "My Mistress, the Desert." A portion tells of his love for the barren wastes:

> She made a desert man out of me in two short
>   lessons,
> and that was just the beginning,
> the beginning of a long line of rendezvous that
>   stretched across
> a long line of years.*

Bob Nolan died of a heart attack on 16 June 1980. As he wished, there were no services. Following cremation his ashes were scattered in a long, straight line over the Nevada desert so his "mistress" could find him there.

*Bob Nolan, "My Mistress, The Desert," *Pioneer News* 10–13 (Spring 1980): 40.

Cool Water

Words and Music by
BOB NOLAN

*Diagrams for Guitar, chord names for Uke & Banjo

32 I'm An Old Cowhand
1936

Johnny Mercer could not read music, but it did not keep him from becoming one of the most prolific and versatile songwriters in the history of American popular music.

John Herndon Mercer was born in Savannah, Georgia, on 18 November 1909. He composed his first song, "Sister Susie, Strut Your Stuff," when he was only fifteen years old. Three years later he went to New York, where he did small roles in several plays.

Johnny attended an audition in New York in 1929 for the Broadway show *Garrick Gaieties* and was told that they needed only girls and songs. He got to work and wrote the song "Out of Breath (and Scared to Death of You)." It was accepted for the revue and sung by Sterling Holloway. During the run of the musical, Johnny met dancer Ginger Meehan, and they were married a year later.

The first big hit for Johnny Mercer was "Lazy-bones," written in 1933 with Hoagy Carmichael. Subsequently he wrote duets for himself and jazz trombonist Jack Teagarden while they were vocalists with the Paul Whiteman Orchestra. Partly as a result of the Mercer and Teagarden recordings, Johnny was called to Hollywood in 1935 by RKO to write, sing, and act in two motion pictures, *Old Man Rhythm* and *To Beat the Band.*

Between movie assignments, Johnny and Ginger took a trip back to Savannah by automobile. It took six days to drive back, three of the days spent crossing Texas. It struck Johnny as somewhat funny to see so many cowboys in spurs and ten-gallon hats driving around in automobiles. In fifteen minutes he put it all into a song he called "I'm An Old Cowhand," written on the back of an envelope in the breezy, vernacular style that was to become a Mercer tradition.* It is one of the few

*Lee Griffin, "Songwriter Johnny Mercer: Still Going Strong at 64," *The Atlanta Journal and Constitution Magazine* (Sunday, 19 May 1974): 54.

Johnny Mercer (ASCAP)

songs for which Johnny Mercer wrote both words and music. He based the melody on the old anonymous song "Westminster Chimes," which in turn was inspired by the clock in the tower of the House of Parliament in London. Big Ben, named for Sir Benjamin Hall, commissioner of works at the time the clock was erected, chimes the quarters on four bells corresponding to the notes B♭, D, C, and F. The sequence has been attributed to George Frideric Handel (1685–1759).*

Bing Crosby introduced "I'm An Old Cowhand" in the Paramount musical *Rhythm on the Range* in 1936 and helped secure a firm foothold in Hollywood for Johnny Mercer as a songwriter. In the meantime Johnny was a vocalist with the Benny Goodman Orchestra in 1938–39 and founded Capitol Records in 1942 with Glenn Wallichs and Buddy De Sylva.

In 1946 Johnny Mercer won his first Academy Award for "On the Atchison, Topeka and the Santa Fe," written with Harry Warren. In 1951 he collaborated with Hoagy Carmichael on another Academy Award winner, "In the Cool, Cool, Cool of the Evening." He took two more Academy Awards in 1961 and 1962 with "Moon River" and "Days of Wine and Roses," both written with Henry Mancini.

During a forty-year career writing songs for motion pictures and contributing to ten Broadway musicals, Johnny Mercer is said to have written 1,000 songs. He helped organize the Songwriters Hall of Fame and became its first president. Their first inductees were named in 1969.

Gene Autry sang "I'm An Old Cowhand" in the 1941 Republic picture *Back In the Saddle*, and Roy Rogers featured it two years later in the Republic picture *King of the Cowboys*.

Johnny Mercer died at his home in Bel Air, California, on 25 July 1976.

*Peter William Dykema, ed., *Twice 55 Plus Community Songs, the New Brown Book, Enlarged to Contain 175 Songs and Choruses with Responsive Readings* (Boston: C.C. Birchard & Co., 1927), no. 113.

Bing Crosby's Sensational Hit

I'm An Old Cowhand
(From the Rio Grande)

From the Paramount Picture "Rhythm on the Range"

Words and Music by
JOHNNY MERCER

I'm An Old Cowhand   157

33 Empty Saddles
1936

John Keirn Brennan, a successful songwriter himself, wrote a poem in 1933 on which Billy Hill later based the popular song "Empty Saddles." Brennan was called "Jack" by his friends, but his poems and song lyrics were written under the by-line J. Keirn Brennan.

Jack Brennan led an adventuresome life as a drifter and wove his experiences and reflections into poetry and song. As a fourteen-year-old in

1887, he worked as a night manager in a local telegraph office in San Francisco. At nineteen he became a cattle buyer for one of the largest ranches in California. Later he drifted to the Yukon and took part in the gold rush.

When he returned from the gold fields, the self-educated musician became an entertainer in Chicago, where he met composer Ernest R. Ball. He moved to New York and teamed with Ball as a lyricist on a number of songs. Their first song for a Broadway show was "A Little Bit of Heaven" in 1914.

The Blue Book of Tin Pan Alley comments that Brennan "punched cows in Texas and panned gold in the Klondike before discovering pay dirt in Tin Pan Alley."* During a twenty-five-year career in New York, Brennan was associated with the Shuberts and with Oscar Hammerstein. He was also a writer for Chauncey Olcott soon after the turn of the century. Brennan songs were featured in four different musicals on Broadway during 1929. Later in the year he moved to Hollywood, working for a short time with Warner Brothers before retiring.

A collection of J. Keirn Brennan poetry about conquistadors, seafaring men, cowboys, Indians, wild geese, and Hawaii was published in 1933 in his book *Trouble-Busters*. The small volume contains a poem entitled "Empty Saddles":

J. Keirn Brennan (Courtesy of Ann Brown)

*Jack Burton, *The Blue Book of Tin Pan Alley* (Watkins Glen, N.J.: Century House, 1950), 1: 250.

160

When composing a song, he worked out the music first and then the lyrics. His beautiful melodies were set to an accent in the rhythm that matched the slow gait of a walking horse, a fitting tempo that became a distinguishing feature of cowboy and western songs.

"Empty Saddles" was a good song title. Hill believed he could retain the subject, rework the words of the Brennan poem, and adapt his own lyrics to music. The result was one of the most beloved cowboy songs in America.

"Empty Saddles" was featured in the 1936 Paramount motion picture *Rhythm on the Range*, starring Bing Crosby with a cast that included Frances Farmer, Bob Burns, and Martha Raye.

J. Keirn Brennan died in Hollywood, California, on 4 February 1948.

Empty saddles . . .
Back from over the border,
Empty saddles . . .
Caught another marauder.
Men . . . Men . . . Men . . . Men!
Ride side by side until they fall.
Saddles creaking,
Filled with rollicking cowboys,
Saddles speaking,
Whisper, "Where are they now, boys?"
Gone . . . Gone . . . On . . .on!
Was their last call.
Guns . . . Guns . . . Guns,
Their only law;
Sons . . . Sons
Of the "forty-four!"
Empty saddles . . .
Gleaming there in the sunlight,
Empty saddles . . .
Dreaming where in a gun fight
Flashing came in the night,
Men who fought for the right,
Then went over the side,
At the end of the ride;
Empty saddles . . .
Call across the Great Divide!*

Billy Hill was riding high as one of the most successful songwriters in Tin Pan Alley in 1936.

*J. Keirn Brennan, *Trouble-Busters* (Hollywood, Calif.: Winston-Brennan Publications, 1933), 53.

Words by
BILLY HILL
From a poem by
J. Keirn Brennan

From Bing Crosby's Paramount picture "Rhythm On The Range"
Empty Saddles

Music by
BILLY HILL

R.E.

34 Twilight On The Trail
1936

What were said to be the two favorite songs of President Franklin D. Roosevelt are both considered cowboy songs despite their origins. One was written in 1873 as a poem with the title "Oh, Give Me a Home Where the Buffalo Roam." The term *range* was used as an infinitive in the poem by Dr. Brewster Higley, its writer, to declare that he would not leave his home "to range," or wander, from his beloved Kansas homestead. The other Roosevelt favorite was "Twilight On the Trail," written in 1936 for a motion picture with a Kentucky mountain setting.

Over the years the word *range* in the early poem came to be used as a noun meaning a cattle range. Now musically known as "Home on the Range," the song is permanently linked with the cowboy. "Twilight On The Trail" was also adopted by the cowboy genre. The song itself was as suitable for the romantic trails cowboys sang about as it was for a logging trace back East. Simulated hoofbeats of the cow horse soon became a distinctive part of musical interpretations and background accompaniments of the song.

The manuscript copy of "Twilight On The Trail," by Sidney D. Mitchell and Louis Alter, as well as a recording of it by Bing Crosby, were both presented to the Roosevelt Memorial Library in Hyde Park, New York, at the request of Mrs. Eleanor Roosevelt.

John Forrest Knight, a former University of West Virginia law student who became a western film comic, introduced "Twilight On The Trail" in the 1936 Paramount film *The Trail of the Lonesome Pine*. The soft, mellow voice of the singer had earlier earned him the nickname "Fuzzy."

The Trail of the Lonesome Pine, starring Sylvia Sidney, Henry Fonda, and Fred MacMurray, was the first outdoor movie ever filmed in color. Two silent screen versions of the backwoods melodrama preceded it in 1916 and 1923. All versions were based on the popular novel by the same name, depicting the poetic side of life in the Kentucky mountains, written by John Fox, Jr., and first published in 1908.

Sidney D. Mitchell (ASCAP)

"Twilight On The Trail" also became the title song in a 1941 Paramount production starring William Boyd, who achieved movie fame as the fictional western hero "Hopalong Cassidy."

The words to "Twilight On The Trail" were written by Sidney D. Mitchell, who teamed with many tunesmiths of the day to produce songs for Hollywood musicals. Mitchell was born in Baltimore, Maryland, on 15 June 1888. He was educated at Baltimore Polytechnic Institute and at Cornell University. He was a newspaper reporter in his hometown for five years before becoming associated with a New York publishing house as a songwriter in 1917. Mitchell moved to Hollywood in 1929 to write songs and special material for films. He died in Los Angeles on 25 February 1942.

The music to "Twilight On The Trail" was composed by Louis Alter, one of the most important songwriters in the history of popular American music. Alter was born in Haverhill, Massachusetts, on 18 June 1902. At the age of nine he began to study the piano, and in four years he was providing the accompaniment to silent films as a pianist in a local theater. He ignored the music cue sheets that came with the films and created his own music to suit the action in the picture. Following his graduation from high school, Alter finished his education at the New England School of Music in Boston. He went to New York City in 1922 as a music accompanist and music arranger. The sounds of the big city inspired him to write "Manhattan Serenade" in 1928, which remains one of the most beloved popular musical compositions of all time. Alter went to Hollywood in 1929, the same year Sidney D. Mitchell moved to the West Coast. Alter divided his time between New York and Hollywood before dying of pneumonia in New York on 5 November 1980.

Featured in the Paramount Picture "The Trail Of The Lonesome Pine"

Twilight On The Trail

Words & Music by
SIDNEY D. MITCHELL
and LOUIS ALTER

Molto Moderato

35

Wah-hoo!
1936

Cliff Friend wrote the music to "Lovesick Blues" in 1922 before he went to Hollywood as a songwriter. The song was a sleeper for twenty-seven years until Hank Williams sang it on the Grand Ole Opry in 1949. (Courtesy of Albert F. "Skip" Friend)

At the close of the Revolutionary War, the great-grandfather of songwriter Cliff Friend homesteaded in the Northwest Territory near the frontier settlement of Losantiville, which later became Cincinnati, Ohio. John Clifford Friend was born on the same farm on 1 October 1893. His seven brothers and two sisters all had musical talent, probably inherited from their father, who played first violin in the orchestra pit of the Woods Theater in Cincinnati.

Cliff Friend learned to play the piano at the age of eight. When he was thirteen he complained

about the talent of the piano player in the Dreamland, a silent movie theater in the Cincinnati suburb of Reading. The manager told the budding young musician if he could do better to go ahead and try. He did and was hired. He borrowed five dollars, walked to downtown Cincinnati, and bought a suit to wear at his new job.

While performing locally, Friend enrolled in the Cincinnati Conservatory of Music. His concert training was interrupted by an advanced case of tuberculosis, which forced him to spend three years in an Arizona sanitorium. When he returned to Cincinnati, he met Harry Richman. As a piano team they played the vaudeville theaters in Ohio, then ended up in California, where they were hired by Al Jolson.

The first popular song hit by Cliff Friend was "You Tell Her—I Stutter," written in 1922 to Billy Rose lyrics. Later in the year, Friend wrote the music to "Lovesick Blues" with words by the Russian-born composer, author, and publisher Irving Mills. With only forty cents in his pocket, Friend sold all rights to the song for $500.

"Lovesick Blues" was a sleeper for twenty-seven years until Hank Williams, billed as "The Drifting Cowboy," made his initial appearance on stage at the WSM Grand Ole Opry in Nashville, Tennessee, on 11 June 1949. The standing ovation Hank received and his half-dozen encores of the song were instrumental in sending it skyrocketing into its place as a country-blues classic.

Between 1921 and 1931, Cliff Friend wrote stage songs and scores for musical revues featuring such stars as Al Jolson, Eddie Cantor, and Jimmy Durante. In 1929 he was called to Hollywood by Fox Films.

Friend's chief collaborator for motion pictures and hit songs between 1936 and 1950 was Dave Franklin. In 1936 they wrote the popular "When My Dream Boat Comes Home" and a year later the novelty favorite "The Merry-Go-Round Broke Down," based on a personal experience in the South.

"Wahoo," a word of widespread Indian usage, was a popular exclamation or yell in the American West in the 1930s. Rodeo contestants often yelled it to attract attention or for the sheer satisfaction of accomplishment.

The *wahu* of the Dakota Indians was the arrowwood or burning bush, known to have cathartic properties. The Sioux made a liquid from the shrub to rid themselves of body vermin. The medicinal *uhawhu*, or wahoo, of the Creek Indians was the southern winged elm. A sap obtained from the bark was used to treat dyspepsia. White men mixed an ounce of the juice with a quart of whiskey to make a quack medicine called Wahoo Bitters. Drinking the concoction usually brought forth a loud verbal reaction that identified the treatment by name. Without the "medicinal" additive, consumption of the liquid base often elicited the same yell. Cliff Friend made the word a national expression of enthusiasm in 1936 with his pseudo-cowboy song "Wah-hoo!" It was featured on "Your Hit Parade" from February through April and was sung by the Andrews Sisters in the Universal motion picture *Moonlight and Cactus* in 1944.

Cliff Friend stayed active in songwriting for many years until a series of heart attacks halted his work. He died in Las Vegas, Nevada, on 27 June 1974.

WAH-HOO!

Words and Music by
CLIFF FRIEND

*Diagrams for Guitar Accomp.

WAH - HOO!
Extra Choruses

The way to Wah Hoo

Oh - you open your mouth - two feet wide
And you take a big breath or two
And then you WAH HOO WAH HOO WAH HOO!
Oh - you wiggle your toes and grit your teeth
Like dangerous Dan McGrew
And then you WAH HOO WAH HOO WAH HOO!
Be careful not to sing soprano
And never Hi-de-hi-de-ho
'Cause that don't go out in Idaho
Oh - buckle your belt and fix your hat
And spit 'er out *(noise)* ka-chew
And then you WAH HOO WAH HOO WAH HOO!

History

Oh - what did Miss Cleopatra say
To Anthony when they met
(crowd)-She hollered WAH HOO WAH HOO WAH HOO!
Oh - what did that roaming romeo
Yell to Miss Juliet
(crowd)-He hollered WAH HOO WAH HOO WAH HOO!
It started way back in Eden
And Eve was the cause and it's no fib
She wahooed Adam for a rib
Oh - what did Miss Pocahontas yell
The minute she saw John Smith
(crowd)-She hollered WAH HOO WAH HOO WAH HOO!

Oh gimme the plains - the western plains
And a bottle of apple jack
And let me WAH HOO WAH HOO WAH HOO!
Oh gimme a saloon - an old spittoon
And a package of chew tobacc -
And let me WAH HOO WAH HOO WAH HOO!
Give me a gal from dear old Dallas
And play a Texas Tommy dance
And I'll cut loose with a wild romance
Oh gimme a gat - a cowboy hat
A handkerchief - red and blue
And let me WAH HOO WAH HOO WAH HOO!

Oh gimme the plains - a pair of reins
And my boots and saddle too
And let me WAH HOO WAH HOO WAH HOO!
Oh lemme get at - a lariat
As a steer comes into view
And let me WAH HOO WAH HOO WAH HOO!
Give me the wide open spaces
Each time I see a sawdust bar
I wanna be away out thar'
Oh show me the pal who'll steal my gal
And hand me my thirty-two
And let me WAH HOO WAH HOO WAH HOO!

Special Orchestra Chorus.
Oh Saxophone man - do what you can
And give me that wah hoo too *(Business by Saxophone)*
Oh you Slide Trombone - give out a moan
With rhythm that's really new *(Business by Trombone)*
Come on you Cornet - get busy
Just blow and push the first valve down
Music goes around and'round
Hey Banjo and Drum - Oh come, come, come
Altogether now WAH HOO WAH HOO WAH HOO!
(Business by entire band)

36 We'll Rest At The End Of The Trail 1936

Cowboy songs were the vogue in 1936. One summer evening, songwriter Fred Rose went over to the Curt Poulton home in Nashville, Tennessee, where he and his friend decided to write a song about a cowboy, his horse, and the hereafter. Fred sat down at the piano and asked, "What are some names cowboys give their horses?" Curt named a few of the more commonly used ones, and they agreed on Old Pal.

The composers spend a long time on the rhyming combinations in the bridge to get the cowboy and his horse within the galaxy of riders once their work on earth was through and they had reached the end of the trail. They kept gropin' around with *hopin'*, *copin'*, and *loafin'*, but finally reached a decision:

If we feel like ropin' we'll hitch to a star,
So just keep on lopin' it's not very far.

Curt Andra Poulton was born in New Martinsville, West Virginia, on 25 February 1907. His wife, Vervia, was also an entertainer. Using the radio name Betty Wagner, she played tenor guitar with Jack Shook, Nap Bastin, and Dee Simmons in a group called the Dixie Dews. Along with Herald Goodman and Dean Upson, Curt Poulton was a member of the original Vagabonds, one of the most popular vocal trios of the early 1930s. All three were sons of ministers. The vagabonds joined the Grand Ole Opry in 1930 after successful stints at WGN Chicago and KMOX St. Louis. The smooth

guitar strumming of Curt Poulton was their only accompaniment.

Knols Fred Rose was a remarkable talent in the country music industry. He was born in Evansville, Indiana, on 24 August 1897 and grew up in St. Louis, Missouri. Fred was a self-taught pianist at the age of seven, and by the time he was ten he was performing before audiences. Four years later he was singing and playing in honky-tonks and

Curt Poulton (Courtesy of Vervia E. Poulton)

Fred Rose (Country Music
Foundation Library and Me-
dia Center)

restaurants in Chicago, which led to a contract
with the Brunswick Record Company. Later on, he
and pianist Fats Waller cut piano rolls for the QRS
Company.

Fred Rose began writing songs at the age of seventeen. His first successes, written while he was
still in his twenties, were songs for the flamboyant
Sophie Tucker, Russian-born star of American
cabarets, burlesque, and vaudeville. They included "Red Hot Mama," "'Deed I Do," and
"Honest and Truly."

During his varied career, Rose teamed with
Elmo Tanner as the Tune Peddlers on KYW Chicago. He and Ray Bargy each played one of the
two white grand pianos in the Paul Whiteman Orchestra, the most popular dance band in America
at that time. By himself, he did a regular CBS network show over WBBM Chicago. From Chicago,
Fred Rose went to Nashville briefly, then on to
New York. In 1940 he was in Hollywood where he
wrote sixteen songs for Gene Autry.

Back in Nashville in 1942, Fred Rose and Roy
Acuff formed Acuff-Rose Publications, the first
publishers in the United States devoted exclu-
sively to country and western music. All the while
Rose continued to write hit songs and help aspiring singers, musicians, and songwriters with their
careers.

Fred Rose was a positive influence on Curt
Poulton after the breakup of the Vagabonds in
1935. Curt had tried it as a single, but when he
returned from World War II with an injured left
hand, he was unable to continue successfully. His
finger pressure was erratic and he would often dub
the tones on his guitar. Rose introduced him to
photography, which became a favorite pastime.

Fred Rose died in Nashville on 1 December
1954. Curt Poulton died of a heart attack in the
same city on 9 November 1957.

In 1961 Fred Rose was one of the first three inductees into the Country Music Hall of Fame along
with Jimmie Rodgers and Hank Williams.

We'll Rest At The End Of The Trail

(Diagrams for Guitar Acc.)

Words and Music by
CURT POULTON and
FRED ROSE

END   OF THE TRAIL.   If   we   feel like rop - in' we'll

hitch   to   a   star,   So   just   keep on lop - in'   it's   not ver - y   far. We're

wear - y   and tired   our   work   is   all thru'.   But WE'LL REST   AT THE

END   OF THE TRAIL.   We're   TRAIL.

37 Oklahoma Hills
1937

Left: Woody Guthrie (Country Music Foundation Library and Media Center)

Above: Jack Guthrie (Country Music Foundation Library and Media Center)

If American protest singer Woody Guthrie could have ridden a horse, he might have been a sidekick in B-grade western movies for his first cousin Jack Guthrie.

The two Guthries were born in the Indian country of Oklahoma: Woodrow Wilson "Woody" Guthrie in Okfuskee County on 14 July 1912, and Leon J. "Jack" Guthrie in neighboring Creek County to the north on 13 November 1915.

When a number of Guthries and assorted relatives invaded southern California in 1937, it was the heyday of the singing cowboy in the Los Angeles area. The songs, however, were not the traditional ones the Guthries had known back in Oklahoma and Texas but were new cowboy love songs, often highlighted with yodels. The close harmony and innovative group yodeling of Hollywood cowboys caused one Woody Guthrie biographer to observe that the town sounded more like Switzerland than Texas.

The ambition of Jack Guthrie, known as "Oklahoma" or "Oke," was to become a singing cowboy star. He wore flashy clothes and could ride a horse. On the other hand, cousin Woody usually wore a ragged hillbilly outfit and had not been on a horse since he fell off one and broke an arm when he was a kid.

Following Jack's resolve, the two went to a nearby stable one day to pick out a mount for Woody to ride in his first rodeo parade. Woody fell off the horse almost immediately and skinned an elbow. Several days later, Jack and Woody rode into Gilmore Stadium as part of a show featuring a number of cowboy acts. Hollywood talent scouts were in attendance as usual. Woody again lost control of his horse, and it charged into a band of Hollywood Indians, scattering bows, arrows, and feathers in all directions and just about ending Jack Guthrie's dream to become a film hero.

On 19 July 1937, Jack and Woody began a radio show on KFVD Los Angeles, called "The Oklahoma and Woody Show." They received no pay, but the program did give them an opportunity to promote their personal appearances. The cousins were soon joined by Maxine "Lefty Lou" Crissman, Jack's sister-in-law. By mid-September, Jack left the show to work full time in the construction business, leaving the radio program to Woody and Lefty Lou. They soon dropped the cowboy format.

One fall day in 1937, Woody was sitting on the back steps of the Crissman home in Glendale strumming his guitar. The kid next door came over and asked him where he was from. Woody answered, "I was born in the Oklahoma hills." The statement lingered in his mind after the boy left and in a few minutes he had assembled his initial reflections and come up with a musical chorus. Woody got up and went inside to write; he had finished "Oklahoma Hills" by radio time that night.*

Woody Guthrie's lyrics were often set to older

*Joe Klein, *Woody Guthrie: A Life* (New York: Alfred A. Knopf, 1980), 87–97, 297.

melodies. "Oklahoma Hills" was written to the tune of a little-known 1899 song by a lesser-known Harry Braisted and Stanley Carter, entitled "The Girl I Loved in Sunny Tennessee." For his most famous song, "This Land Is Your Land," Woody borrowed the tune to the earlier "Little Darling, Pal of Mine."

Around 1940 Woody abandoned the hillbilly image and moved to New York, where his repertory became more radical.

Jack Guthrie recorded "Oklahoma Hills" for Capitol Records in 1944 and entered the army soon after. The record was released in June, two weeks before he went overseas. On Iwo Jima, he burned his leg badly and was hospitalized.

During World War II, Woody Guthrie spent some time working in the Merchant Marine. He was drafted into the army in July 1945 and sent to Scott Field near Alton, Illinois. While in the post PX the following month, he was shocked to hear a jukebox recording of "Oklahoma Hills" by his cousin Jack. Somewhat angered by what he thought was Jack's inconsiderateness, Woody began negotiations with Capitol Records for a share of the royalties to the song, which he began to receive two years later.

Jack Guthrie gained considerable fame as a country music singer after the war. His career was interrupted in mid-1947 when he entered U.S. Veterans' Bureau Hospital No. 102, in Livermore, California, a former center for the treatment of tuberculosis. He died there six months later, on 15 January 1948, at the age of thirty-two.

In the 1950s, a debilitating family disease, Huntington's chorea, began slowly destroying Woody Guthrie's physical stamina, but from a hospital bed he continued to spread his influence and write songs about the homeless, trade unions, sharecroppers, migrants, and textile workers. The legendary folk balladeer died in the Creedmoor State Hospital in Queens, New York, on 4 October 1967.

OKLAHOMA HILLS

Key of F (C-D)

By JACK GUTHRIE
& WOODY GUTHRIE

38 Old Buck-A-Roo 1937

A few old-time cowboys told their stories for someone to put down on paper as Teddy Blue Abbott did. At age seventy-eight he recalled his past and projected his hopes for the future: "Only a few of us are left now, and they are scattered from Texas to Canada. The rest have left the wagon and gone ahead across the big divide, looking for a new range. I hope they find good water and plenty of grass. But where ever they are is where I want to go."* In 1939, less than a year later, Teddy Blue himself had "left the wagon."

An old buckaroo whose boots and saddle have been put aside, leaving him with only fleeting memories, is the subject of the poignant "Old Buck-A-Roo," written in 1937 by one of the most versatile, yet least known, songwriters in America. Fleming Allan Smith was born on 2 February 1904, or, as he liked to say, "on ground-hog day," and he died sixty-one years later to the day. The native South Dakotan grew up in an atmosphere rich in anecdotes and lore of the open range, herds of buffalo, and the Indian war-whoop. Both of his grandfathers grew up in Dakota Territory when Sitting Bull, Wild Bill Hickok, Calamity Jane, Preacher Smith, and Poker Alice were colorful contemporary characters.

Fleming Allan Smith studied music at the University of Pennsylvania and became a theater organist in Chicago. He later was musical director

Fleming Allan (*WLS Family Album*, 1934)

for opera singer Madame Schumann-Heink and a close friend of bandmaster Lawrence Welk.

In 1931 Smith returned briefly to Sioux Falls, South Dakota, to receive accolades for composing "Diamond Jubilee March" to help celebrate the seventy-fifth anniversary of the town. He wrote the song under the name Fleming A. Smith. For his songwriting career, however, he was to drop his surname.

*E. C. "Teddy Blue" Abbott and Helen Huntington Smith, *We Pointed Them North: Recollections of a Cowpuncher* (New York: Farrar & Rinehart, 1939), 256–70.

As musical director of the WLS Chicago "National Barn Dance" from 1931 to 1933, and on the production staff of the Chicago NBC Studios during the two years following, Fleming Allan was closely associated with early western performers like Gene Autry, Smiley Burnette, Pat Buttram, Patsy Montana, Louise Massey, "the little cowboy" Georgie Gobel, and the Dean Brothers—Jimmy and Eddie—whom he had recruited in Omaha, Nebraska.

Fleming Allan went to Hollywood in 1935 to write for western films. He published 227 songs, which fill a number of folios and are liberally scattered throughout countless others. His favorite was "I've Sold My Saddle For an Old Guitar."

Gene Autry sang "Old Buck-A-Roo" in two movies. The first was the 1937 production *Public Cowboy Number 1*, and in 1952 he did an encore in *Barbed Wire*.

The printing history of "Old Buck-A-Roo" is unusual. Three different song folios by M. M. Cole Publishing Company of Chicago and one by a subsidiary all have the last name of the composer misspelled Allen. In 1937 the song was published in a small format folio, *50 Favorite Songs of "Peewee King" and the Original Golden West Cowboys*, with two four-line verses. A year later, "Old Buck-A-Roo" appeared in another small folio, *Songs of the Range*, printed by the Belmont Music Company of Chicago, an M. M. Cole subsidiary.

The chorus of "Old Buck-A-Roo" was printed without verses in 1939 by M. M. Cole in a large folio, *The Ranch Boys' Songs of the Plains*. The most complete version of the cowboy song was published in 1942 in a large format by M. M. Cole Publishing Company with an eight-line verse in *Song Favorites of WSM Grand Ole Opry*.

For the last ten years of his life Fleming Allan headed Music Country Trends, his own publishing company in Los Angeles. He died unheralded, in relative obscurity, and almost penniless on his birthday in 1965.

OLD BUCK-A-ROO

Featured by Stacy Sisters

Words & Music by
FLEMING ALLEN

39 Back In The Saddle Again 1938

A monumental influence on American cowboy songs at home and abroad has been radio, record, motion picture, and television star Gene Autry. During his career he revived cowboy ballads, wrote his own cowboy songs, and gave worldwide exposure to compositions of other songwriters.

Gene was born Orvon Gordon Autry on 29 September 1907 in Tioga, Texas, the son of a cattle buyer and grandson of a Baptist minister. Ranch life and service in a local church choir were to play an important part in his life as a singing cowboy. As a young man, Gene helped drive cattle to the railroad station where he became interested in trains and telegraphy. He learned Morse code and eventually became the chief telegrapher in Chelsa, Oklahoma.

To pass the lonely night hours in the railway office, Gene bought a guitar and learned to play it. It was into the Chelsa railway office that cowboy humorist Will Rogers came one summer night in 1929 to send a wire. He heard Gene singing and encouraged the young man to pursue a singing career in radio. Three weeks later Autry traveled to New York by train in quest of fame and fortune, but he was advised that he needed more professional experience.

When Gene returned to Oklahoma, he got a job on KVOO radio in Tulsa. Not long after, he returned to New York and recorded his own composition, "That Silver Haired Daddy of Mine." The phenomenal success of the record earned him a Columbia Records contract and an eventual spot on "National Barn Dance" out of WLS Chicago.

In 1934 film producer Nat Levine of Mascot Films signed Gene to a contract, and he left Chicago for Hollywood. He did three supporting roles, the first two with cowboy star Ken Maynard, before his big break came in 1935 with his first starring role in *Tumbling Tumbleweeds*. "America's Singing Cowboy" was in the saddle.

Paralleling Gene Autry's career was that of singing cowboy Ray Whitley. Between 1936 and 1956, Ray appeared in fifty-four films and was a successful recording artist and songwriter. Raymond Otis

Gene Autry (Courtesy of Gene Autry)

Ray Whitley (Saturday Matinee)

a tune to it. He told Kay he would add a "whoopee-ti-yi-ya" or something like that when he got to the studio.*

Ray Whitley introduced "Back In The Saddle Again" in *Border G-Man* and recorded it later in 1938 with the Six Bar Cowboys for Decca Records.

In 1939 Ray and Gene Autry reworked the song for the Autry movie *Rovin' Tumbleweeds*. The following year Gene needed a theme song for his CBS radio show "Melody Ranch." He was urged to use the title song from his 1940 motion picture *Melody Ranch*, but Gene decided on "Back In The Saddle Again."

Ray Whitley died while on a fishing trip in Mexico on 21 February 1979. He often gave credit to the one who helped him with "Back In The Saddle Again." He believed that the song would have been just another western tune had it not been for his friend Gene Autry.

*Gerald F. Vaughn, *Ray Whitley: Country-Western Musicmaker and Film Star* (Newark, Del.: Shamrock Printing Co., 1973), 4.

Whitley was born on 5 December 1901 in Atlanta, Georgia, and he grew up in Alabama. While working on the construction of the Empire State Building in New York City in 1930, Ray organized a musical group called Ray Whitley and His Range Ramblers and began a regular radio show on WMCA. The following year he appeared regularly at the famous Stork Club. In 1932 he landed a job as a musical entertainer with the traveling World Championship Rodeo organization. In appreciation for the employment, he renamed his group the Six Bar Cowboys, honoring the Texas ranch of the rodeo director.

In 1938 Ray Whitley was under contract with RKO Radio Pictures as a co-star in George O'Brien movies. On the morning that he was to prerecord the songs for the film *Border G-Man*, he got a call at 5:00 A.M. from one of the studio executives, telling him that they had a place for another song if he could come up with one by 7:00 A.M. Ray went back to the bedroom, told his wife, Kay, the studio wanted another song, and added, "I'm back in the saddle again." Kay told him what he had just said was a good title for a new song, so he sat down on the edge of the bed and wrote a verse and made up

Back In The Saddle Again

Words and Music by
RAY WHITLEY
and GENE AUTRY

*Names of chords for Ukulele and Banjo.
Symbols for Guitar.

40 Dust 1938

When the cast and film crew of Republic Studios went on location to Lone Pine in the High Sierras of California in 1938 to film *Under Western Stars*, the first motion picture starring Roy Rogers, they needed a song about a dust storm scheduled to be filmed in the picture. Songwriter and veteran entertainer Johnny Marvin provided the plaintive cowboy classic and nature supplied the dust storm. A wind machine, taken along to create a big blow, turned out to be excess baggage when a sudden wind storm blew so hard during the filming of the scene that it nearly blew the actors off their horses.

Dust has always been a problem for cowboys. Exposed not only to major dust storms and whirling dust devils, old-time cowboys were choked and almost blinded by the dust raised by moving herds. Cattle, horses, and men often became mere silhouettes in the thick clouds of dust that burned under the scorching sun of the plains. "Rocks in the beans and sand in the meat" was a common lament sung during the old trail-driving days, and drovers on the Painted Desert of Arizona had to keep one hand over the top of their coffee at mealtime to keep the wind from blowing it out of the cups.* Dust was inevitable.

John Senator Marvin was born on 11 July 1897 in a covered wagon three miles south of Butler, Oklahoma. Early publicity on Johnny reported that he was born on the Ozark Mountain Trail and was not sure if the event happened in Oklahoma, Missouri, Arkansas, or Kansas. According to his parents, however, they were near their destination in Curtis County, where they would stop and buy a small ranch.

At the age of ten Johnny began playing the guitar at country dances while his father played the fiddle. Two years later he ran away from home to join a circus. After two years of roaming around, he returned home and eventually opened up a barber shop in Butler. But wanderlust was still in him. In

Johnny Marvin (Courtesy of Gloria Fleming)

*Glenn R. "Slim" Ellison, *Cowboys Under the Tonto Rim* (Tucson: University of Arizona Press, 1968), 163.

Bowlegs, Oklahoma, Johnny dyed his hair, darkened his skin, and joined a traveling group called the Royal Hawaiians, replacing a member who had just died. He learned to play the ukelele and the steel guitar and stayed with the group as their fourth member until World War I, when he joined the U.S. Navy.

After the war, Johnny Marvin went into vaudeville, billed as Honey Duke and His Uke. His career took him to New York City in 1920s as an entertainer on radio and records. For five years he had his own daily network radio show on NBC. In the meantime, he found time to do a singing role in the 1926 musical *Honeymoon Lane*, in which singer Kate Smith made her Broadway debut.

Johnny Marvin was joined in New York by his brother Frankie in 1929 and the two befriended young Gene Autry, who was in the big city in quest of a record contract. Later they joined Autry in Hollywood. Johnny became a songwriter and producer of the "Melody Ranch" radio show and wrote eighty songs for Gene Autry movies.

The Johnny Marvin entertainment troupe in New England in the early 1930s, appearing under the auspices of the William Morris Agency of New York. *Left*, guitarist Eddie McMullen; *center*, Gloria Price, who became the wife of Johnny Marvin; *right*, Johnny Marvin. (Courtesy of Gloria Fleming)

Johnny Marvin accompanied comedian Joe E. Brown on a twelve-week tour of the South Pacific military bases in 1943, providing live entertainment for American fighting men. In the Papuan jungles, where the show troupe was only a six-minute march from Japanese positions, Johnny contracted dengue fever and had to be flown out of New Guinea to a hospital in New Zealand for treatment. He never fully recovered from the jungle disease, which limited his show work and other activities. He died on 20 December 1944 in North Hollywood, California, of a heart attack.

Dust

(Diagrams for Guitar Acc.)

Words and Music by
JOHNNY MARVIN

41 San Antonio Rose
1938

Bob Wills and His Texas
Playboys in 1940. This is the
famous "San Antonio Rose"
band. *Left center*, Bob Wills.
(Country Music Foundation
Library and Media Center)

James Robert Wills was born one minute before
midnight on 6 March 1905 on a farm near
Kosse, Texas. He learned Negro folk music and
rhythms while working with blacks as a youth in
Texas cotton fields. At the age of ten, young Jim
Rob, as he was then called, played the fiddle at his
first ranch dance when his fiddle-playing father
failed to show up.

Wills moved to Fort Worth in 1929 and began playing the fiddle with guitarist Herman Arnspiger on three different radio stations. The two called themselves the Wills Fiddle Band. The following year they added other musicians. In 1931 they became the Light Crust Doughboys and began a prime-time radio show for the Burrus Mills and Elevator Company, with W. Lee O'Daniel, president and general manager of the company, serving as their announcer.

In 1933 most of the band members moved with Wills to Waco and changed their name to Bob Wills and His Playboys. When the group moved to WKY Oklahoma City the next year, they added Texas to the name. KVOO Tulsa beckoned in late 1934, and there Bob Wills put together one of the best dance bands in America, combining western and swing music.

The term "western swing" is synonymous with Bob Wills and His Texas Playboys. Unlike other dance bands of the day, the Wills group featured the steel guitar, fiddle, and other stringed instruments along with the standard brass and reeds of big bands. It was a unique combination of frontier fiddle music and jazz.

In late 1938 Bob Wills and His Texas Playboys recorded "San Antonio Rose" as an instrumental number in Dallas. The Wills composition, with fiddle and steel guitar lead, became a big hit.

Early in 1940, Irving Berlin, Incorporated, of New York, contacted Wills with an offer to publish "San Antonio Rose." The music was forwarded to the publisher without lyrics because none had been written. The company provided lyrics about a cowboy singing to a low-hanging prairie moon and assuring his Alamo sweetheart that he would ride back to her when the roundup was over. The song went to press.

Meanwhile, Bob Wills and some of his band members put their heads together and came up with their own words to the song. Everette Stover, a trumpet player in the group, probably helped Bob more than anyone else, although Sleepy Johnson, vocalist, also contributed. The finished lyrics were then sent to the New York publisher.

On 16 April 1940, Wills and what has been called the "San Antonio Rose" band of eighteen members recorded the song again, complete with the folk cry and ad-lib trademarks of Bob Wills. This time the song contained the Wills lyrics and bore an altered title, "New San Antonio Rose." The record gained popularity throughout America before the sheet music with unauthorized lyrics came out. When the printed version did become available in stores, buyers were dismayed to find out that the words were not the ones in the Wills recording, and in alarming numbers they demanded their money back. The publisher had to go back to press with the Wills lyrics and recall thousands of printed copies with the company lyrics that had been rejected by the public. Imprinted on the previously designed cover for "San Antonio Rose" was the short vindication "The New and Original." The song made its composer a national musical figure.

A 3–4 December 1973 recording session of Bob Wills and His Texas Playboys was set to coincide with their reunion in Dallas. It turned out to be the last session for the band with their leader. An ailing Bob Wills was there on the first day and led the band from a wheel chair. Occasionally he let loose with his famous "ahhh-haaa." That night he slipped into unconsciousness and was practically lifeless the next day when the band recorded "San Antonio Rose." Hoyle Nix hollered for Bob and all eyes in the studio filled with tears. The album of twenty-four songs was appropriately titled *Bob Wills and His Texas Playboys For the Last Time*.

Bob Wills died on 13 May 1975, nearly eighteen months later, without ever regaining consciousness.

The New and Original
San Antonio Rose

By BOB WILLS

+) Symbols for Guitar, Chords for Ukulele and Banjo.

42 Leanin' on the Ole Top Rail
1939

"Leanin' on the Ole Top Rail" made an appearance on "Your Hit Parade" on 9 March 1940, as one of the top ten songs in the nation, and probably no one in Forsyth, Montana, knew that it had been composed in their midst. The cowboy standard could not have been created in a more appropriate setting.

Herds of cattle from Texas began to arrive in the area in 1882 to thrive on the free grass of Montana. The town of Forsyth had its beginning a year later when the Northern Pacific Railroad reached the junction of the Yellowstone River and Great Porcupine and Little Porcupine creeks, where the company purchased land for a division point. It soon became one of the early "queen cities of cowland." Cowboys joined the beaver men, buffalo hunters, and Indian fighters as a part of the colorful history of the area, one of the last strongholds of the Indian and the buffalo.

In 1939 New York composer-violinist Charles Kenny was making a cross-country trip by car. His brother Nick had given him a song title to work on in case he became inspired while in the West. Nothing happened until he stopped for a night in Montana. Forsyth was like a ghost town. Kenny fell asleep and awoke the next morning with a melody running through his mind. It sounded strangely familiar to him but it fit the title he had been given.

Once Kenny had the tune going, the rest of the song came easy. But he still was vaguely worried by a feeling he had heard part of the melody before. Maybe it was on the car radio, he thought, or perhaps at one of the eating places where he had stopped. It bothered him.

After finishing the song, Kenny got into his car and headed west. It was not long before he found out where he had filched the tune. His attention was drawn to a western meadowlark pouring its

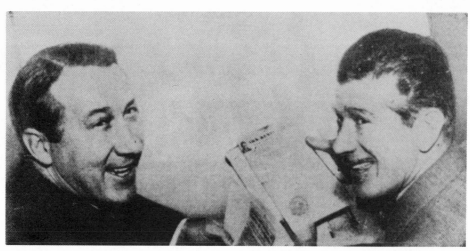

Nick and Charles F. Kenny
(Courtesy of Nick Kenny)

heart out on the top rail of a wooden fence, and the notes matched the opening bars Kenny had just blended into song.

The songwriting Kenny brothers were both from Astoria, Long Island City, New York. Their father was an Irish tenor from County Cork, and their mother was a French-Canadian contralto. Nicholas Bonaparte Kenny was born on 3 February 1895, and Charles Francis Kenny was born on 23 June 1898. Open seas and smoke-filled newspaper offices were both a big part of their lives. The brothers were in the U.S. Navy aboard the USS *Arizona* during World War I. Nick was in charge of the newspaper on the battleship and frequently printed his own aphorisms, which he called Kennygrams.

Nick Kenny worked for newspapers in New Jersey and Massachusetts before going to the New York *Daily Mirror* as a reporter and columnist in 1930. In the meantime he was writing lyrics to hit songs and pioneering radio production by establishing one of the first radio amateur hours.

Charles Kenny began writing songs while in the navy and kept writing through eight trips to South America in the merchant marine. He too joined the *Daily Mirror* and remained for twenty-six years as a radio and television columnist until the newspaper folded in 1963.

Nick and Charles Kenny teamed together in writing such hit songs as "Love Letters in the Sand," "While a Cigarette Was Burning," "It's a Lonely Trail When You're Traveling All Alone," and "Gone Fishin'." "Your Hit Parade" status for "There's a Gold Mine in the Sky" in 1937 gave the brothers a name for their business house—Goldmine Music, Incorporated. Nick Kenny died on 1 December 1975 in Sarasota, Florida.

By the writers of "THERE'S A GOLD MINE IN THE SKY"

LEANIN' ON THE OLE TOP RAIL

Words and Music by
NICK KENNY and
CHARLES KENNY

Stars are graz-in' in the mead-ow of the sky, Moun-tains lie in slum-ber deep, All the range has an-swered na-ture's lull-a-by But there's a lone-ly gal who can-not sleep.

43 South of the Border
1939

On 8 November 1939, the *New York Times* printed a story from a special correspondent with British forces in France that troops all up and down the front lines were singing the doleful U.S. ballad "South of the Border." Why the song had become a favorite of British soldiers was puzzling to the reporter. "It has nothing to do with England, France or war," he explained.*

Although the song had been introduced earlier in the year by "America's Singing Cowboy," Gene Autry, while he was on an extended tour in the British Isles, it was not of U.S. origin. Near the start of the tour, two local songwriters had visited Autry in his dressing room between shows in Dublin and presented him with "South of the Border," a British product they had written for the star in the hope that he would record it. Autry liked the song and incorporated it in his remaining shows overseas.

Composers Michael Carr and Jimmy Kennedy had never been to Mexico, but they had seen Gene Autry movies with ranchos and vaqueros and believed that most of the films had been shot south of the border. Michael Carr was not new to cowboy songs. He had collaborated five years earlier with Hamilton Kennedy, Jimmy's brother, to produce "Ole Faithful."

When Gene Autry returned to America with "South of the Border," Republic Pictures bought

the song for $1,000, had a script written, and filmed the movie *South of the Border* before the year ended. In 1943, still retaining rights to the song, the studio produced *Down Mexico Way*, using the second line of the song lyrics for the film title.

Jimmy Kennedy was one of the great songwriters of modern popular music and has been called "the doyen of Britain's Golden Age author-composers." He was born on 20 July 1902 in Armagh, Northern

Jimmy Kennedy (Courtesy of Ian Whitcomb)

*"Doleful U.S. Ballad Is the Favorite At Front; British Troops Singing 'South of the Border,'" *New York Times*, 8 November 1939.

Michael Carr (Courtesy of
Jimmy Kennedy)

London. Jimmy Kennedy died at the age of eighty-
one on 6 April 1984 in Cheltenham.

"South of the Border" made quite an impression
on Gene Autry. When asked in 1983 to reveal his
happiest memory in show business, he replied:

> When I was on tour of England and Ireland, I
> played the Dublin Theatre for two weeks. The
> people were so warm and friendly that after
> each show I'd walk outside behind the theater
> and sing a song or two to a few dozen who
> would be waiting.
>
> My last night when I went outside, there were
> around 100 there. I sang "South of the Border,"
> and they hummed along with me. Then, just as
> I started to leave, they sang "Come Back To
> Erin." It was such a spontaneous and sincere
> outpouring of affection that I've never forgotten
> that night.*

*Reba and Bonnie Churchill, "Gene Autry: One of the First
Singing Cowboys Is Still No. 1 in Many Ways," *Grit* 16 (27 March
1983): 3.

Ireland. After his graduation from Dublin University, he became a schoolmaster. His first effort at
songwriting in 1931 resulted in "The Barmaid's
Song," a successful comedy chorus for holiday
crowds at Blackpool.

In 1934 Jimmy Kennedy's publisher turned down
one of his songs and released it to Peter Maurice
Music Company, Ltd., of London. The rejected
"Isle of Capri" became the first world hit song for
his new publisher. Jimmy Kennedy then began to
turn out such hits as "Red Sails in the Sunset,"
"My Prayer," "Harbour Lights," "Ten Pretty Girls,"
"Serenade in the Night," and "Roll Along Covered
Wagon." He became a cornerstone in the Kennedy-
Carr songwriting team, and they collaborated on
three London Palladium shows, *OK For Sound,
London Rhapsody,* and *The Little Dog Laughed.*

In 1939 the songs "South of the Border" and
"My Prayer" became big hits in the United States.
At the same time Captain Jimmy Kennedy was performing both of his songs with British armed forces
at the front.

Michael Carr, well-known songwriting partner of
Jimmy Kennedy, died on 16 September 1968 in

SOUTH OF THE BORDER
(Down Mexico Way)

By JIMMY KENNEDY
and MICHAEL CARR

Moderato (*serenade*)

BOR - DER ____ Down Mex-i-co way ____ She was a

pic - ture ____ In old Span-ish lace ____ Just for a

ten - der while I kissed the smile up - on her face ____ For it was "Fi-

es - ta" ____ And we were so gay ____ SOUTH OF THE

44

Where The Mountains Meet The Sky 1940

The wide sweep of Arizona's unseasonably hot Painted Desert and the cool, inviting upward thrust of the snow-capped San Francisco Peaks inspired the popular Aston "Deacon" Williams cowboy song "Where The Mountains Meet The Sky."

Aston Parker Williams, nicknamed "Deacon" when he was twenty years old, was born near Avery, Texas, on 1 December 1913. As a youth he traveled as a revival singer with an evangelist preacher. Later he went into popular music. Interrupting a tour while a member of the Al Jennings

Billy Williams, "that Singin' Man"

Orchestra, Williams went back to his hometown for a short visit in 1933. Another revival was in progress and he agreed to lead the singing. When Williams rejoined the touring orchestra and told his fellow musicians how he had spent his time off, they christened him "Deacon."

"Where The Mountains Meet The Sky" was written in 1940 while the talented entertainer was driving alone from Texas to California. It was a blistering summer day on the multicolored desert. Williams kept glancing at the high country on the distant blue horizon and suddenly realized how cool it would be up there where the mountains met the sky. Knowing he could only reach the place by horseback, he started putting the song together as a cowboy would tell the story. The words came easily, and when he arrived in California Williams was surprised that he had retained the melody he hummed while he made up the song.

In early 1942, while playing saxophone and singing with Bobby Pope's orchestra in Kansas City, Williams made an acetate recording of "Where The Mountains Meet The Sky" with the piano man in the band. Also playing Kansas City at the time was Sammy Kaye and His Orchestra. Williams took the recording of his song to George Ginjell, road manager for the Kaye organization, and asked him to play it for the bandleader. Sammy Kaye not only bought the song, but he hired Williams to sing with his orchestra and changed the first name of his new vocalist to Billy.

Sammy Kaye recorded "Where The Mountains

Billy Williams, with the guitar, in the 1947 Columbia Picture *Smoky River Serenade*. (Saturday Matinee)

Meet The Sky" in 1942, as did Horace Heidt and His Musical Knights, Art Kassell and His Kassels in the Air, and other popular dance bands.

As a member of the "Swing and Sway with Sammy Kaye" aggregation, Billy Williams appeared in the 1941 United Artists' picture *Song of the Open Road*, starring Edgar Bergen, Jane Powell, and W. C. Fields. He stayed with the orchestra five years.

In 1947 Billy Williams played the co-starring role of a singing ranch foreman in the Columbia western movie *Smoky River Serenade* with a cast headed by Paul Campbell and Ruth Terry.

"That Singin' Man" Billy Williams formed his own orchestra in the 1950s. It has been described as one of the finest small bands ever assembled and is highlighted by the tenor sax talents and easy singing style of Billy Williams, the former Aston "Deacon" Williams of songwriting fame.

(I'm Headin' For The Blue Horizon)
Where The Mountains Meet The Sky

Words and Music by
ASTON "DEACON" WILLIAMS

45 Along the Santa Fe Trail 1940

The Santa Fe Trail was embedded across the landscape of the American West and in the annals of history by the ruts of freighters, stagecoaches, and covered wagons, as well as by the hoofprints of Indian ponies, pack mules, oxen, cavalry mounts, and Texas cattle. Although primarily a commercial trade route between Missouri and the lucrative markets in the Southwest from 1821 to 1880, parts of the cross-country Santa Fe Trail also felt the tread of cattle as nearly all northbound drives intersected the path at various points.

The Goodnight-Loving Trail, opened in 1866 to move cattle from Texas to Cheyenne, actually followed a portion of the Santa Fe Trail. The cattle course ran west from Texas over the arid Staked Plains, into New Mexico Territory to avoid Comanche Indians, and then up the Pecos River to Las Vegas. Here the cattle trail merged with the mountain section of the Santa Fe Trail and moved through Raton Pass into Colorado and beyond. Partly because of a toll of ten cents per animal through the pass, imposed at his roadhouse by former mountain man and scout "Uncle Dick" Wooten, some later drives skirted the Sangre de

Will Grosz (Courtesy of Ian Whitcomb)

Al Dubin (Courtesy of Patricia Dubin McGuire)

222

Cristo Mountains on the east and followed part of the Cimarron Cutoff of the Santa Fe Trail before veering to the north.

Lyrics to the song "Along the Santa Fe Trail" paint a vivid image. It was composed in 1940 by songwriters Will Grosz and Al Dubin, with Edwina Coolidge given partial credit for the lyrics.

Dr. Wilhelm Grosz was a Jewish composer and conductor who fled Adolph Hitler's Germany and became a writer of popular songs in England and in the United States. He was born in Vienna on 12 August 1894 and began a career as a classical pianist at the age of eighteen. He moved to England in 1934, where he composed popular English songs with Jimmy Kennedy. Their "Isle of Capri," "Red Sails in the Sunset," and "Harbour Lights" all became American favorites. Music for the latter two was written by Grosz under the pen name Hugh Williams so that his royalties would not go to Austria. Grosz came to the United States in April 1939 and signed with Warner Brothers to write songs for motion pictures. He died of a heart attack in less than a year, on 10 December 1939 while playing the piano at the home of friends in Forest Hills, New York.

Al Dubin was born on 10 June 1891, in Zurich, Switzerland, and was named Alexander Dubin after Alexander the Great. He was nicknamed "Alick" by his family, but to generations of American music lovers he was Al Dubin. His anticzarist

father fled Russia and stopped in Switzerland for schooling. The family arrived in the United States in 1896. Al Dubin was destined to become one of America's most popular song lyricists. After four successful Broadway show credits and a number of hit songs, he went to Hollywood in 1929 to write for Warner Brothers.

When the sheet music to "Along the Santa Fe Trail" was published, Edwina Coolidge was named co-lyricist. Sometimes known as Edwina Perrin, she was the daughter of Gladys Perrin, a private nurse of Al Dubin during his shuttles back and forth between Hollywood and New York. Already married, Dubin could not marry Edwina even though he wanted to. He returned to Hollywood with her and her mother in 1940 to write the lyrics to "Along the Santa Fe Trail" for the motion picture *Santa Fe Trail*.

To ensure financial sucurity through royalties for his girlfriend, Dubin gave her credit as a collaborator. By late 1943, however, their long relationship was over. In the biography of Al Dubin, his daughter Patricia summed up the end of the song story: "Al eventually asked Edwina to sign a release with Warner Brothers, for an undisclosed sum of money, revoking all interest in the song 'Along the Santa Fe Trail,' though her name still appears on the sheet music."*

Dubin and another composing partner, Harry Warren, received Academy Awards in 1935 for the song "Lullaby of Broadway." Dubin died on 11 February 1945 in New York City.

*Patricia Dubin McGuire, *Lullaby of Broadway* (Secaucus, N.J.: Citadel Press, 1983), 152.

ALONG THE SANTA FE TRAIL

From the Warner Bros. Picture
"SANTA FE TRAIL"

Words by
AL DUBIN, A.S.C.A.P.
& EDWINA COOLIDGE

Music by
WILL GROSZ
A.S.C.A.P.

The crim-son col-ored can-yon and the az-ure sky, are beau-ti-ful to see 'til

you come pass-ing by, and then they all fade a - way._____

*Diagrams for Guitar, Symbols for Ukulele and Banjo

46 The Call Of The Canyon 1940

The 1921 novel *The Call of the Canyon* by Zane Grey and the 1940 western song "The Call Of The Canyon" by Billy Hill are identical in title and similar in romantic theme. A young soldier in the Grey novel survives an attack of poison gas in World War I and returns from France. He leaves New York for the therapeutic climate of Arizona to regain his health, leaving behind the girl to whom he is engaged. A year later the New York socialite goes to visit her fiancé, intent on taking him back East. No longer is there a sad, hopeless look in his

Billy Hill (ASCAP)

eyes, and gone are the pallid cheeks and deep facial lines he had when he returned from the war. He is wide-shouldered and heavy limbed, and his smooth, bronzed face radiates health and contentment.

After an extended stay in which she is unable to talk her lover into returning to New York, the girl goes back home despite his appeal for her to stay. She soon becomes disillusioned with the city and a subtle call from the canyon keeps beckoning her. As the story goes:

> She becomes haunted by memory pictures and sounds and smells of Oak Creek Canyon. As from afar she saw the great sculptured rent in the earth, green and red and brown, with its shining, flashing ribbons of waterfalls and streams. The mighty pines stood up magnificent and stately. The walls loomed high, shadowed under the shelves, gleaming in the sunlight, and they seemed dreaming, waiting, watching. For what? For her return to their serene fastness—to the little gray log cabin.*

The same age-old motif of one lover waiting for another to return was used by Billy Hill in his composition "The Call Of The Canyon." Before the lovers' parting, the flame of a campfire had been symbolic of a love they vowed would never die.

*Zane Grey, *The Call of the Canyon* (New York: Harper and Brothers, 1924), 221.

Standing alone by the ashes, the one left behind wonders if a love between the two still burns. A tiny spark ignites with a whisper, signaling an affirmative answer to the call of the canyon.

Billy Hill wrote his first song, "Rock-a-Bye Your Baby Blues," to Larry Yoell lyrics in 1927, but his first published song was "They Cut Down the Old Pine Tree," written two years later to his own lyrics. For financial reasons, he wrote "Prairie Lullaby" in 1932 for Jimmie Rodgers, "America's Blue Yodeler." Not wanting to be associated with country music, however, he had changed his name to George Brown. Ironically for Billy Hill, his name is a perfect spoonerism for "hillbilly."

Billy Hill recognized a vast difference between country music and western music. His daughter Lee recalled, "[He] just didn't want to be connected with hillbilly music. He wrote genuine western and the comparison rankled him."* Nationwide acclaim came to Billy Hill in 1933 with his first hit, "The Last Round-Up." Obviously proud of the song, he dropped the pseudonym George Brown.

By 1940 the financial woes that had plagued Billy Hill from the beginning of his songwriting career were over, and he must have again felt the call for travel and adventure. During the last year of his life he spent much time alone, steeped in melancholia. He lived in the city, but his heart was in the land of the cowboy. While in one of his low-spirited moods, he wrote "The Call Of The Canyon," his last published song. It quickly caught the attention of some of the top dance bands of the day. Kay Kyser, Guy Lombardo, and others recorded it for dancing, as well as for listening audiences. It made the prestigious "Your Hit Parade" on 12 October 1940.

Gene Autry sang "The Call Of The Canyon" in his motion picture *Melody Ranch* in 1940. Two years later the song was the inspiration for the title and plot of another Gene Autry movie, *Call of the Canyon*.

During the later part of his songwriting career,

Billy Hill was referred to as the "Modern Stephen Foster." He died in a Boston hotel on Christmas Eve in 1940 after enjoying success as a composer for only seven years. Yet he lived long enough to become one of the foremost of all cowboy and western songwriters.

*Lee DeDette Hill Taylor, "Billy Hill Story" (Valencia, Calif., 1974), typescript, 10 pp.

The Call Of The Canyon

By BILLY HILL
A.S.C.A.P.

It's may-be just the mur-mur of the night wind Or the sigh-ing of the leaves I hear Or the moon-light on the stream that

em - ber   Burn - ing from the days gone   by?

Then I hear a lone - ly whis - per   As a lit - tle spark   I

see   It's THE CALL   OF THE CAN - YON

Bring - ing back your an - swer to   me.   me.

rall.

The Call Of The Canyon   233

47 My Adobe Hacienda 1941

Victoria Louise Massey was born on a Hart County ranch in northeastern Texas on 10 August 1902. When she was an infant, the family moved across the state to Midland. Their next move was to New Mexico, where her father, Henry Massey, acquired the old K Bar outfit in the Capitans of historic Lincoln County, where Billy the Kid had ridden roughshod only three decades before.

When Louise was only fifteen years old, she married Milton Mabie of Roswell, New Mexico, whom she had met while he was having an ice-cream soda in a local drugstore. Instead of losing a member of their musical group with the marriage, the Masseys gained another talented family member.

The Massey Five began with a father, two sons, a son-in-law, and a daughter. Their list of instruments sounds like a music store inventory: accordian, vibraphone, piano, organ, guitar, banjo, violin, bass viol, saxophone, mellophone, mandolin, trumpet, trombone, tuba, and drums. They were truly westerners and featured original songs, authentic cowboy ballads, and love songs of the ranchlands.

The early musical group played and sang mostly for church socials and local talent shows until 1928, when they were heard by the head of the Horner Conservatory in Kansas City. The result was a two-year vaudeville tour of the United States and Canada on the Chautauqua circuit as well as broadcasts over KMBC in Kansas City.

Louise Massey (Pecos Valley Collection, Chaves County Historical Museum, Roswell, New Mexico)

The elder Massey retired to his K Bar Ranch in 1930. Louise Massey, her brothers, Dott (Curt) and Allen, and her husband, Milt, added Larry Wellington, a Californian, to their act. They were called to WLS Chicago in 1933 and became favorites throughout America to fans of the "National Barn Dance" along with such acts as the popular

The original "My Adobe Hacienda" on the banks of the Rio Hondo near the community of Picacho, New Mexico.

Patrick Barrett segment called Uncle Ezra's Station—E-Z-R-A, "the powerful little five-watter down in Rosedale, the friendly little city." Radio listeners kept writing letters to the station manager about "those westerners," so the group adopted the name their fans gave to them.

In 1935 Louise Massey and the Westerners moved to New York for the weekly NBC network radio program "Show Boat." The following year, they became regulars on the NBC-WJZ network show "Log Cabin Dude Ranch."

On annual trips back to New Mexico, Louise and Milt looked for a place to build a home where they could settle down once their professional careers were over. Sitting one day alongside the Rio Hondo near the community of Picacho and looking across the river valley, Louise and Milt agreed that was the place.

A three-room adobe building, built by padres from Old Mexico in 1896, was on the spot that Louise wanted for a hacienda. She and Milt bought the place from the Bloom Land and Cattle Company and started making plans for their home. Instead of tearing down the old building, they decided to add to it.

Back in New York, Louise started working on a song about her dream place. In 1941 she finished "My Adobe Hacienda." Before she could perform the new song on NBC, however, she had to have the music written down. A talented young Polish boy from California, Lee Penny, a friend of the Masseys but not professionally connected with them, prepared the song for publication in three days, and Louise gave him printed credit for his contribution.*

"My Adobe Hacienda" became one of the top seven songs in America as determined by "Your Hit Parade" on 3 May 1947, and ran for ten consecutive weeks. It was the number 2 song on three different occasions.

Louise Massey Mabie died in San Angelo, Texas on 22 June 1983.

*"Louise Massey Recalls Past," *Historical Roundup* 2, no. 1 (Winter 1980): 5.

MY ADOBE HACIENDA

Words and Music by
LOUISE MASSEY and
LEE PENNY

Piano Arr. by Larry Stanton

48 Cimarron 1941

The Bell Boys, Scotty Harrell, Jimmy Wakely, and Johnny Bond, on radio station WKY Oklahoma City in 1938. (Courtesy of Scotty Harrell)

Cyrus Whitfield Bond was an Oklahoman by birth. He was born on 1 June 1915, in the small village of Enville, halfway between Oklahoma City and Dallas, Texas. After starting out his musical career with a ninety-eight-cent Montgomery Ward ukulele, Bond moved to Oklahoma City and was soon broadcasting on radio station WKY with Jimmy Wakely, a future singing cowboy star of motion pictures. In 1937 the two entertainers, along with Scotty Harrell, formed the singing Cowboy Trio and began radio programs sponsored by the Bell Clothing Company on WKY Oklahoma City

238

and KVOO Tulsa. They soon became known as the Bell Boys. Another name change came the same year when Bond adopted the first name Johnny.

While on WKY, the Bell Boys opened their shows with an upbeat, rollicking cowboy tune. Johnny had an idea to write a new musical opener. For a long time he had wondered why the popular 1931 western movie *Cimarron*, starring Richard Dix and Irene Dunne, had no featured song by the same name. In their travels the singing trio had crossed and recrossed the Cimarron River many times and had often commented that a song should be written about this cattle-country river. One day in 1938, Johnny Bond sat down in his bachelor room at the YMCA in Oklahoma City and composed "Cimarron," a new song for radio and personal appearances of the trio.

The Cimarron River was well known and respected by cowboys in the old days. Northbound herds forded the rolling river and fought its treacherous quicksand during the heyday of the storied cattle drives to markets. Drovers sometimes called it the Red Fork of the Arkansas.

The Bell Boys made a trip to Hollywood in 1939 to appear in the Roy Rogers movie *Saga of Death Valley*. They returned to California in June 1940 and three months later began a career as the Jimmy Wakely Trio on the Gene Autry CBS "Melody Ranch" radio show. In the meantime Dick Reinhart had replaced Scotty Harrell as the tenor singer, but the two changed back and forth intermittently until the trio disbanded in the mid-1940s. In movies the trio was frequently billed as Jimmy Wakely and His Roughriders.

"Cimarron" was the first song performed by the Jimmy Wakely Trio after they joined the Gene Autry radio program, and they presented it in the 1941 Bill Boyd picture *Twilight on the Trail* and again in the 1942 Autry film *Heart of the Rio Grande*. Jimmy Wakely recorded "Cimarron" in his first Decca recording session. Les Paul and Mary Ford made a hit record of it for Capitol, and the Billy Vaughn Orchestra topped a million records sold with a Dot recording.

In 1941 Johnny Bond signed his own record contract with Okeh/Columbia and recorded with a musical group he called the Red River Valley Boys. He became a headliner on "Hollywood Barn Dance" on CBS Radio in 1943 and stayed with the program until its cancellation in 1947. In 1953 he joined cowboy movie star Tex Ritter as a script writer-performer on the "Town Hall Party" that aired on NBC Radio and the new television station KTTV in Los Angeles. The popular show was broadcast from the old Town House Building in Compton, near Long Beach, until its closing on 14 January 1961. The composer of some three hundred songs, writer, producer, humorist, and singing sidekick of second-feature western movies died on 12 June 1978.

Cimarron
(Roll On)

By JOHNNY BOND

gray. _____ Tho' I'm feel - in' blue, _____

I'll roll on with you _____ To the

o - cean blue, _____ CIM - AR - RON ROLL

ON _____ ON

★ This number can be played either as written or in fast double time.

49 The Cowboy Serenade
1941

Richard Edward Hall excelled in just about everything he did. This native Coloradan was born in Denver on 3 May 1914. Although he planned to be a medical doctor when he entered Colorado College, it was his hobbies of music and writing that gained him considerable acclaim.

As an undergraduate in college, Rich Hall was known for his musical compositions, including "Chapel Bell" and other campus songs. He was elected captain of the baseball team in 1937, climaxing a year of versatility rarely equaled by a college student. He was president of the Question Club and of Phi Delta Theta, held offices in the interfraternity council and the glee club, was sports editor of the school newspaper, managed the homecoming dance, and was editor of the campus yearbook. In addition, he found time to write both score and script for the rollicking musical comedy *Rhythmic City*, said to be the best student-produced show in the history of Colorado College at that time.

While vacationing in Colorado, Vincent Youmans, songwriter for many Broadway shows, saw one of the three musicals written by Hall while he was a student. He advised the gifted young writer to consider seriously a musical career. Following his graduation from Colorado College, Rich Hall moved to Hollywood and became a staff writer for Warner Brothers. Later he joined the West Coast staff of the Columbia Broadcasting System. In 1939 his song "Once In a Lifetime" was premiered

Rich Hall (Courtesy of Barbara Hall)

nationally by Martha Mears and John Conte on the "It Happened In Hollywood" radio show.

After two years in Hollywood, Rich Hall returned to Colorado for a brief vacation. Re-inspired by the tranquillity and beauty of open ranges and blue skies in his home state, he wrote "The Cowboy Serenade." It is the song of a cowhand smoking his last cigarette and talking to his old paint horse before he rides off to the purple hills to meet a lady love "where the good green pastures are grown."

"The Cowboy Serenade" was introduced on the radio in 1941 by singer Tony Martin. On the night of the broadcast an offer to publish the song, accompanied by an advance check, was received by the composer from the Edward B. Marks Corporation in New York.

Convinced that the song captured the spirit of the West as few others did, Kay Kyser and His Orchestra recorded "The Cowboy Serenade" in 1941, and before the year was over so had the big bands of Gene Krupa, Art Jarrett, Glenn Miller, and Russ Morgan. During its initial period of popularity "The Cowboy Serenade" was recorded by ten different dance bands and by such noted vocalists as Barry Wood and Roy Rogers. Gene Autry featured "The Cowboy Serenade" in his 1942 Republic Picture *Cowboy Serenade*, co-starring Smiley Burnette and Fay McKenzie.

The Rich Hall composition "Blue Afterglow" was introduced by the Glenn Miller Orchestra on CBS in 1941. In addition to his songwriting, Hall also wrote for the Groucho Marx "You Bet Your Life" television show.

Composer Rich Hall's untimely death came on 5 June 1965 at his home in Van Nuys, California.

The Cowboy Serenade

(While I'm Smokin' My Last Cigarette)

Words & Music by
RICH HALL

While I'm smok - in' ____ my last cig-ar - ette ____ Sing that

cow - boy song I nev - er will for - get ____ Yip - ee - ky -

smok - in'_____ my last cig-ar - ette_____ Come on old Paint, this

time we're trav-'lin' a - lone_____ Gon-na meet her where the good green past-ures are

grown_____ So while twi - light_____ and pur-ple hills fade_____

_____ From a camp-fire comes that COW-BOY SER-E - NADE_____

246   The Cowboy Serenade

50 Jingle Jangle Jingle
1942

"Jingle Jangle Jingle" was written in early 1942 for a motion picture, but it became a nation-wide hit song before the movie was released. A recording by Kay Kyser and His Orchestra sold more than a million discs, and the song achieved the top ranking in America by mid-July.

The cheerful western song, written in a jocular style, made its first appearance on "Your Hit Parade" in the number 5 position during the radio broadcast of 4 July 1942. The following week it made number 4, the next week number 3. On 25 July, "Jingle Jangle Jingle" became the number 1 hit song in nation and held the position for five weeks. It was in contention for fourteen straight weeks.

The nonmusical motion picture *The Forest Rangers*, starring Fred MacMurray and Paulette Goddard, was released in October. "Jingle Jangle Jingle" was featured in the film as a serious song despite its lightheartedness.

During World War II, General Elliott Roosevelt named his B-17 Flying Fortress the "Jingle Jangle" and adopted the popular composition as the theme song for his squadron.

"Jingle Jangle Jingle" was composed by Hollywood songwriters Joseph J. Lilley and Frank Loesser for Paramount Pictures. It was written in the two-voice canon form with exact repetitions of preceding parts in the same key.

Joseph J. Lilley's career spanned the era of big bands, radio, and musical movies. For more than twenty-five years he was on the musical staff of Paramount Pictures. Lilley was born in Providence, Rhode Island, on 16 August 1914. At age ten he began taking piano lessons from a nun at St. Teresa's School in Providence. Six years later he became the pianist for the Billy Lossez Orchestra aboard a Boston-to-New York pleasure boat.

While still a teenager Lilley attended the Boston Conservatory of Music and the Juilliard School of Music. He played and arranged music for night-club singers in New York City, including Dorothy

Frank Loesser (ASCAP)

Meyer and Eddie DeLange in 1936. This took Loesser to Hollywood, where he wrote "Moon of Manakoora" the following year for the movie *The Hurricane*. His lyrics were written for some of the most eminent composers in Hollywood. He often wrote the words before the composers had written the music. Several of his collaborators urged him to write music also.

Based on a statement supposedly made by a navy chaplain during the Japanese attack on Pearl Harbor in 1941, Loesser wrote both words and music to a song for the first time. "Praise the Lord and Pass the Ammunition" became the first major song hit of World War II.

In addition to a successful Hollywood career, Loesser was highly acclaimed as a composer on Broadway with such hit musicals as *Where's Charley?*, *Guys and Dolls*, and *The Most Happy Fella*.

Loesser's Academy Award–winning song "Baby, It's Cold Outside," in the 1949 movie *Neptune's Daughter*, was written in the two-voice canon form used earlier in "Jingle Jangle Jingle."

Loesser died in New York City on 28 July 1969. Joseph Lilley died in Hollywood on 2 January 1971.

Lamour, who encouraged him to go into radio. After serving as a vocal coach and music supervisor for the National Broadcasting Company in the 1930s, Joseph Lilley moved to Hollywood as a musical director for Paramount. He worked on movies that starred Bing Crosby, Bob Hope, Dean Martin and Jerry Lewis, Betty Hutton, and Danny Kaye.

Because he wrote tunes for torrid love scenes in two Paramount films, both starring Loretta Young, Lilley became known as an expert on "sex music." The dubious honor caused him to remark in 1948, "It's getting to the point where I've become a western picture fan. Romance is barred in the sagebrushers and I'm fed up with love scenes."*

Francis Henry Loesser was born on 29 July 1910 in New York City. He shortened his first name, which he detested, and dropped the middle one entirely when he was a boy. Frank Loesser came from a musical family but never studied music formally. He learned to play the piano by ear and soon began to write verses and song lyrics. After submitting some of his best work to Leo Feist, young Loesser was hired to write lyrics for fifty dollars a week.

The first successful song for Loesser was "I Wish I Were Twins," written to the music of Joseph

*O'Toole, [news release,] Paramount Pictures, Hollywood, Calif., 1 December 1948.

(I GOT SPURS)
Jingle Jangle Jingle

Words by
FRANK LOESSER

Music by
JOSEPH J. LILLEY

*Dedicated to the Pico Stables
Burbank, Calif.*

*Chord Names for Guitar

Piano Arr. by Geo. N. Terry

51 Along the Navajo Trail
1942

Larry Markes and Dick Charles were page boys at the NBC Studios in New York City during late 1940, each making $90 a month. Directing their talents to writing songs, the two came up with a number of blues, including the popular "Mad About Him, Sad Without Him, How Can I Be Glad Without Him Blues." Another blues melody, published under the title "Prairie Parade," was introduced in 1942 in the Columbia picture *Laugh Your Blues Away*, starring Bert Gordon and Jinx Falkenburg.

Bandleader and composer Eddie DeLange (ASCAP)

Lou Levy, president of Leeds Music Corporation in New York and the husband of singer Maxine Andrews, was not satisfied with the title "Prairie Parade." The alliterative *p*s sometimes popped when sung into a microphone, making the words inaudible. Levy asked for a new title and the necessary changes in the lyrics. A friend of the publisher, bandleader Eddie DeLange, came up with the title "Along the Navajo Trail" the next day. Levy liked it and offered to publish a revision under the new title if the composers would agree to share credits and royalties with DeLange. They were hesitant about the deal, but Levy cautioned, "Remember boys, two-thirds of something is better than three-thirds of nothing." Markes and Charles finally agreed after Levy promised them a recording of the song by Bing Crosby and the Andrews Sisters. Through their own efforts, however, Dinah Shore was the first to record it under the new title.

The original Navajo Trail was used by Navajos to drive horses, cattle, and sheep east over colorful wastelands for trade with Pueblo Indians, victims of early Navajo raids along the Rio Grande. The Navajo stock was exchanged for beads and other goods to improve their silversmithing and blanket weaving. The trail was also used as a mail-stage route and by wagon trains that furnished supplies for troops and Indian agents.

From deep in the Navajo country of Monument Valley and Canyon de Chelly in northeastern Arizona Territory, the Navajo Trail led eastward through the San Juan Valley, by Fort Defiance and Gallup, over the Continental Divide east to San

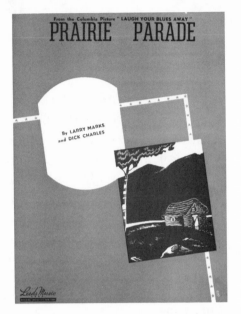

Dinah Shore, Larry Markes, and pianist Dick Charles share a song. (Courtesy of Dick Charles)

Below: Cover of sheet music for "Prairie Parade" by Larry Marks and Dick Charles, from the Columbia Picture *Laugh Your Blues Away*. Published by Leeds Music Corporation.

Mateo, alongside Cabezon Peak, then skirted the Jemez Pueblo and headed into Santa Fe.* Other trails used by the nomadic traders were called by the same name.

Lawrence Wolcott Markes, Jr., a highly decorated fighter-bomber pilot during World War II, was born in Brooklyn, New York, on 24 September 1921. In addition to being a songwriter, he became a successful writer for radio and television. While stationed in England in 1945, Markes was unaware that "Along the Navajo Trail" had been featured that year in a Roy Rogers motion picture by the same name. Markes and a British girlfriend attended a showing of the film in London. When the song came on, the astonished composer blurted out, "I wrote that song!" Satisfied that Markes was trying to impress her, the girl replied, "Oh, that's alright Yank. I like you anyway."

Richard Charles Krieg used only his given names

for his professional career. Dick Charles was born in Newark, New Jersey, on 24 February 1919. He became a successful radio producer-director and was fortunate enough to have bandmaster Paul Whiteman help him get started. For many years he headed the Dick Charles Recording Service in New York.

Edgar DeLange, born on 12 January 1904, in Long Island City, New York, was an orchestra leader during the big band era. He helped form the Hudson-DeLange Orchestra in 1936, and collaborated with his partner on the successful song "Moonglow." With Duke Ellington he wrote the popular "Solitude." DeLange moved to Hollywood in the late 1940s and wrote for motion pictures until his death on 13 July 1949.

*Carl Eickemeyer, *Over the Great Navajo Trail* (New York: Press of J. J. Little, 1900), 15–27.

ALONG THE NAVAJO TRAIL

Key Eb (C - Eb)

By LARRY MARKES
DICK CHARLES
EDDIE DE LANGE

52 Sioux City Sue 1944

Dick Thomas and Max C. Freedman in 1946. (Courtesy of Dick Thomas)

Richard Thomas Goldhahn was born on 14 September 1915, in Philadelphia. The future singer of cowboy songs rode plow horses on a family farm as a young man and dreamed of someday riding the wide open spaces of the American West on a real cow horse.

In 1934 Goldhahn began singing over WPEN Philadelphia as a yodeling cabin boy on the radio show "S.S. All in Fun." For his professional career he dropped his family name and became Dick Thomas.

In 1941 Thomas and his family moved to California, where he worked in western motion pictures, had his own radio show on KFWB Hollywood, and appeared on the "Lamplighter" show over the Mutual Network.

In July 1943, Thomas returned to the East Coast because of World War II to await his induction into the armed forces. During the interim he went to work at the Village Barn in New York City and frequently wrote catchy song lyrics about girls and places like "The Beaut from Butte," "My Alice

Down in Dallas," and "I Lost My Gal From Galveston on the Sidewalks of New York."

Thomas played and sang nightly over the radio from the Village Barn over WOR and the Mutual Network. On 1 April 1944 he recorded eight cowboy songs that were purchased by National Records, a new company. Thomas passed his physical for the U.S. Army a week later and took his family to Philadelphia to prepare for going into the service.

In the early fall of 1944, Thomas met part-time Philadelphia composer and author Max C. Freedman at the post office at Thirtieth and Market Street where Freedman was a clerk. Thomas told his new acquaintance about his songwriting lyrics on girls and places. In response, Freedman confided that he would like to write some cowboy lyrics and get an opinion of them.

Thomas soon received lyrics for several songs, but his busy schedule forced him to set them aside. He glossed over the lyrics two months later and again put them aside, all except an eight-verse poem entitled "Sioux City Sue." He metered it in short order and wrote the words to a chorus, adding "Your hair is red, your eyes are blue, I'd swap my horse and dog for you." Thomas used the title five times in a chorus that was only sixteen bars long, even though it was unheard of to do such a thing at that time. He adapted three Freedman verses to the melody and finished the song.

Thomas played "Sioux City Sue" for Freedman and his wife Rachel on 9 January 1945 at their apartment and was disappointed at their lack of enthusiasm. He then went to National Records in New York, where the song was approved for recording along with seven others. He brought songwriting contracts back to Philadelphia, but Freedman was reluctant to sign, preferring an ASCAP (American Society of Composers, Authors and Publishers) publisher. Thomas assured him that National would become ASCAP eventually. Still undecided, Freedman suggested that his wife sign the contracts, so Rachel entered her nickname Ray alongside that of Dick Thomas as co-writer.

Dick Thomas recorded "Sioux City Sue" on 5 February 1945, and he was inducted into the U.S. Army a week later. The record was released, and by September "Sioux City Sue" was listed by *Billboard* magazine as the number 5 folk record in America (the list included only the top five at that time). The record rose to number 1 in November. Others recorded the song, and it stayed in the top five until the end of July 1946. During the week of 6 March 1946, recordings of "Sioux City Sue" by four different artists held four of the six top spots as the most-played jukebox folk records in the nation.

A Bing Crosby Decca record released in early March 1946 had a lot to do with pushing "Sioux City Sue" into the pop charts and on to the Lucky Strike–sponsored "Your Hit Parade" for fourteen weeks.

Republic Pictures purchased the rights to "Sioux City Sue" as a film title, and Gene Autry made it his first movie after being discharged from the U.S. Army Air Force.

Max C. Freedman was co-writer of the rock music milestone "Rock Around the Clock" with Jimmy DeKnight (James E. Meyers) in 1953. He died in Philadelphia on 8 October 1962.

SIOUX CITY SUE

Lyrics by
RAY FREEDMAN

Music by
DICK THOMAS

CHORUS

SIOUX CIT-Y SUE, ———— SIOUX CIT-Y SUE, —

———— Your hair is red, your eyes are blue, I'd

swap my horse and dog for you. SIOUX CIT-Y SUE,—

———— SIOUX CIT-Y SUE,———— There ain't no gal as

true as my sweet SIOUX CIT-Y SUE. ———— SUE. ————

53

The Everlasting Hills
Of Oklahoma   1947

A large part of Oklahoma is hill country. In the western part of the state, the barren Antelope Hills rise above the high plains alongside the Great Western Trail, an outlet for northbound trail herds in the 1880s and 1890s. Farther east, as the elevation drops to the central lowlands, are two major hill groupings separated by the rolling Red Beds region that runs north and south across the state. In west-central Oklahoma are the Gypsum

Hills, capped with a layer of earth containing large quantities of the white component; in the east-central part of the state are the mineral-rich Sandstone Hills. Parts of this lengthy chain of hills support the Cross Timbers, a dense strip of scrub oak forest separating the short-grass plains from the woodlands of eastern Oklahoma. North of the Arkansas River in northeast Oklahoma lie the Osage Hills. East and slightly south are the Indian Hills, Western Hills, and Cookson Hills.

It was on the plateau of northeast Oklahoma, in the green, wooded hills of the old Cherokee Nation, that one of the original Sons of the Pioneers spent a good part of his youth. Vernon Harold "Tim" Spencer was born in July 1908 on Friday the 13th in Webb City, Missouri, a mere ten miles from the Oklahoma and Kansas borders. The Spencer family was large enough to have two male quartets, which often performed together as a single group. Their father was a musician who played the violin in a local symphony orchestra and played the same instrument as a fiddle at country dances. Two years after Tim's first public singing performance at the age of three, the family moved to northern New Mexico and homesteaded a section of land near the Sangre de Cristo Mountains. The pioneer living conditions in the rugged unspoiled backcountry made a lasting impression on young Tim Spencer.

Within two years, the majority of the Spencer family moved back near Tim's birthplace, this time to the small community of Picher in the Oklahoma

Tim Spencer (Saturday Matinee)

hills. The historically significant locale lay in the path of the East Shawnee Trail, the earliest established cattle trail used by Texas drovers to move herds north to railheads for shipment to markets. The ever-present hills inspired Tim to write what he considered his finest composition, "The Everlasting Hills Of Oklahoma."

In pursuit of a musical career, Tim Spencer left for California in 1931 and moved in with his brother Glenn in Los Angeles. In the fall of 1932, Tim joined Bill "Slumber" Nichols and Leonard Slye (Roy Rogers) as a replacement for Bob Nolan in the Rocky Mountaineers, a western music group. When Nolan returned a year later, he, Slye, and Spencer organized the Pioneers Trio, the original name of the Sons of the Pioneers.

The great songwriting team for the Sons of the Pioneers was composed of Tim Spencer, his brother Glenn, and Bob Nolan. Their original songs and the inimitable singing style of the performing members established the identity of an organization often referred to as "The Aristocrats of the Range."

The Spencer family and where they lived were an inspiration to Tim and his songwriting. The old Santa Fe Trail, which threaded through the immediate area of their New Mexico homestead, inspired the imposing composition "Over the Santa Fe Trail." One night after hearing his father tell of the slow trek in a wagon train from his home in Illinois, Tim wrote "Westward Ho!"; he later honored his mother with "That Pioneer Mother of Mine." Bob Nolan helped him write the haunting "Blue Prairie." Once when a motion picture was changed in the middle of the shooting, Tim composed "The Timber Trail" in two hours.

Tim Spencer left the Sons of the Pioneers in 1949 to spend more time with his own music publishing company, although he still managed the group until 1952.

Tim Spencer and his wife, Velma, were two of the founders of the nondenominational Hollywood Christian Group that included Roy Rogers and Dale Evans and flourished in the 1950s and 1960s.

Religious songs written by him and issued by his publishing house, Manna Music, include "The Circuit Ridin' Preacher," "Cowboy Camp Meetin'," and "Lie Low, Little Doggies [sic]" with its poignant recitation. His most popular composition is the 1949 heart song "Room Full of Roses."

Tim Spencer died at his home in Apple Valley, California, on 26 April 1974.

The Everlasting Hills Of Oklahoma

Words and Music by
TIM SPENCER

Slowly

1. THE EV - ER-LAST-ING HILLS OF O-KLA-
2. EV - ER-LAST-ING HILLS OF O-KLA-

HO - MA,___ They hold a mil - lion treas-ures to be found, Gold-en grain on
HO - MA___ Are told in cloud-ed stat - ues in the sky, Pi - o - neers who

hills of green Wave to val - leys cool and clean, Too bad some folks have nev-er seen THE
long have gone, Their wa-gon wheels still rum-ble on, When thun-der peals and falls up-on THE

EV-ER-LAST-ING HILLS OF O-KLA-HO-MA.

2.-3. The

ev-er-last-ing fame of O-kla ho-ma____ Will live in names of men she claimed her own;

Some were right and some were wrong, In his-t'ry's pag - es, prose and song, Oh hail them now for they

all be - long To THE EV-ER-LAST-ING HILLS OF O-KLA-HO-MA.

54 Blue Shadows On The Trail
1947

In 1947 Johnny Lange and Eliot Daniel were commissioned to write songs for one of the six segments in the Walt Disney animated musical motion picture *Melody Time*. Lange was hired to write the lyrics. Daniel, already under contract at Walt Disney Studios, was asked to supply the music.

Sometime later Johnny Lange drove with his wife, Helen, from Hollywood to their place in Palm Springs so he could relax and read the script at his leisure, hoping to dream up a few basic lyric ideas for two cowboy songs.

Following dinner a few days later, Johnny made himself comfortable on a lounge chair by the swimming pool and started reading the movie script. After about twenty minutes he stopped to rest his eyes and became mesmerized as he gazed at the starry skies. A beautiful moon was casting reflections, and blue shadows covered the mountains. Before him were vast stretches of sand and long winding trails that seemed never to end. The sight of all this grandeur instilled in his heart a feeling that gave rise to the simple images and lines that later were to be an integral part of "Blue Shadows On The Trail."

Blending the music of Eliot Daniel and the lyrics of Johnny Lange, the songwriters prepared a demonstration record with piano and voice. They inserted a whistle in a lyrical pause following the opening phrase. Then, more or less as a gag, they tried a coyote howl. Disney liked the idea, and the wild cry stayed in the picture.

Eliot Daniel works with a singer at a show given for the military near the end of World War II. (Courtesy of Eliot Daniel)

In the last segment of *Melody Time*, the mood for "Blue Shadows On The Trail" was brilliantly interpreted on film with the appearance and harmony of the Sons of the Pioneers set against a backdrop of desert views at night.

John Logo was born of Italian parents in Phila-

Helen and Johnny Lange in 1974. (Courtesy of Johnny Lange)

delphia on 15 August 1909. For his songwriting career, he changed his name to Johnny Lange. The versatile composer created songs of all types, including cowboy, western, love, gospel, animal, Christmas, Irish, French, Hawaiian, and Spanish, and songs about legendary American characters. Lange moved to Hollywood in 1937 to write for motion picture studios and, by his own admission, did not know a dogie from a dog when he started writing about cowboys. In 1949 he helped write the popular frontier freighter song "Mule Train."

In addition to writing the music for the Pecos Bill segment of *Melody Time*, Eliot Daniel was one of the two music directors for the entire film. Eliot Howard Daniel was born in Boston on 7 January 1908. He was educated at Boston Latin School, Harvard University, and Harvard Business School. Daniel was in the radio and recording business for eleven years before joining the U.S. Coast Guard during World War II. In 1945 he moved to Hollywood and became composer-conductor for Walt Disney Studios. The word "blue" became a lucky one for Eliot Daniel. Less than two years after "Blue Shadows On The Trail," his composition "Lavender Blue" received an Academy Award nomination.

From Walt Disney's "Melody Time"

Blue Shadows On The Trail

Words by
JOHNNY LANGE

Music by
ELIOT DANIEL

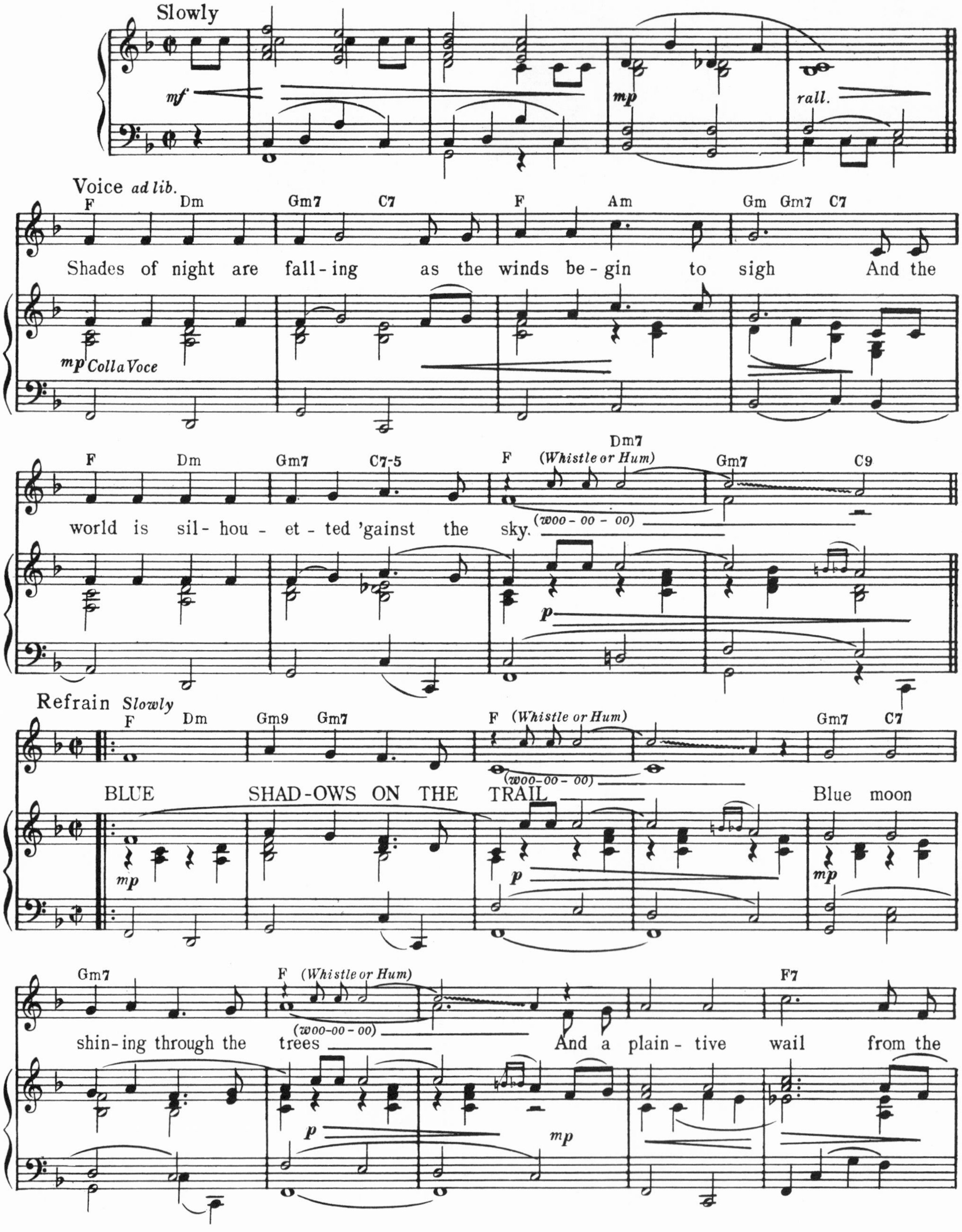

Slowly
mf
mp
rall.
Voice ad lib.
F Dm Gm7 C7 F Am Gm Gm7 C7
Shades of night are fall-ing as the winds be-gin to sigh And the
mp Colla Voce
F Dm Gm7 C7-5 F (Whistle or Hum) Dm7 Gm7 C9
world is sil-hou-et-ted 'gainst the sky. (woo-oo-oo)
p
Refrain Slowly
F Dm Gm9 Gm7 F (Whistle or Hum) Gm7 C7
BLUE SHAD-OWS ON THE TRAIL (woo-oo-oo) Blue moon
mp
p
mp
Gm7 F (Whistle or Hum) F7
shin-ing through the trees (woo-oo-oo) And a plain-tive wail from the
p
mp

55 Pecos Bill 1947

Wild as the West Texas wind are the tales about Pecos Bill, mythical giant of the cattle country who rode a mountain lion and carried a live rattlesnake for a whip.

Pecos Bill was born in Texas when it was an independent nation. His pioneer mother, who once killed forty-five Indians with a broomstick, weaned Bill on moonshine at the age of three days. It is said that he and Paul Bunyan were brothers, but it can't be proved. There's no doubt, though, that they were both fathered by a liar. When a family located fifty miles away from where Bill was born, his father decided that the place was getting too crowded, so he upped and moved west. With seventeen or eighteen children in the wagon, nobody noticed that baby Bill had fallen out when they crossed the Pecos River. He was raised by coyotes, learned their language, and had fleas. He lived this way until a cowboy convinced him that he wasn't a varmint. Even Bill could figure out he didn't have a tail.

Bill could ride anything. Once he climbed on an Oklahoma cyclone at the Kansas line and rode it down across Texas. The Staked Plains was heavily timbered until this big wind wiped it bare. But Bill wasn't thrown. The cyclone simply rained out from under him. This was what washed out the Grand Canyon, although some say Bill dug it in one week while prospecting. He came down in California and lit in what is now Death Valley. The impact drove the place down more than a hundred feet below sea level, and the imprint of his hip pockets is still visible on the baked surface of the basin. Bill indirctly had a hand in the naming of the Painted Desert. One day he scared a band of Indians so badly their warpaint fell off and turned a drab Arizona landscape into a thing of beauty.

How Pecos Bill died is a matter of argument. Some say liquor wasn't strong enough for him and he started drinking nitroglycerine. Others say he started putting fishhooks and barbed wire in his toddy and they eventually rusted out his innards, sending him to his infernal reward.*

A musical tribute to Pecos Bill was written in 1948 by Johnny Lange and Eliot Daniel for the Walt Disney extravaganza *Melody Time*. The talented songwriters also created the hauntingly beautiful "Blue Shadows On The Trail" for the same production.

While sitting beside a campfire on the desert during the final sequence of the feature movie, a young boy asks Roy Rogers why coyotes howl at the moon. Through the Disney technique of combining real people and animated cartoon characters, the singing cowboy and the Sons of the Pioneers explain in story and song how Pecos Bill was raised by coyotes and has an undivided love for his horse Widowmaker—undivided, that is, until he meets the winsome cowgirl Slue-Foot Sue. On their wedding day, Sue makes the mistake of insisting that she be allowed to ride the horse, who hasn't liked her from the start for coming between him

---

*Edward O'Reilly, "The Saga of Pecos Bill," *Century Magazine* 106, no. 6 (October 1923): 826.

"Ridin' that lion a hundred feet at a jump, and quirtin' him down the flank with the rattlesnake"

and Bill. The wonder horse easily throws Sue, and when she lands on her big spring bustle, she bounces up into the air. Every time she comes down, she rebounds higher and higher. Finally in outer space, she heads toward the moon and never comes back down. A heartbroken Pecos Bill, according to the story, returns to his coyote brothers, and every night they howl at the moon for his bouncing bride, poor Slue-Foot Sue.

Pecos Bill (*Century Magazine*, October 1923)

From Walt Disney's "Melody Time"

Pecos Bill

Words by
JOHNNY LANGE

Music by
ELIOT DANIEL

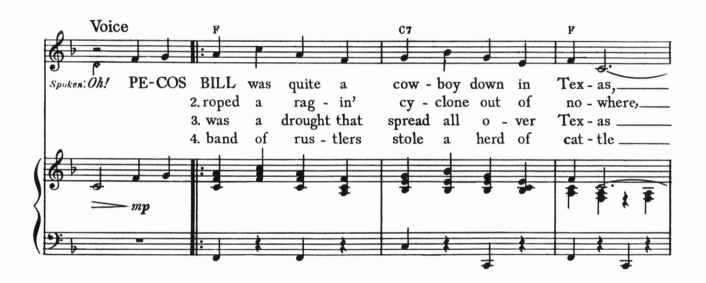

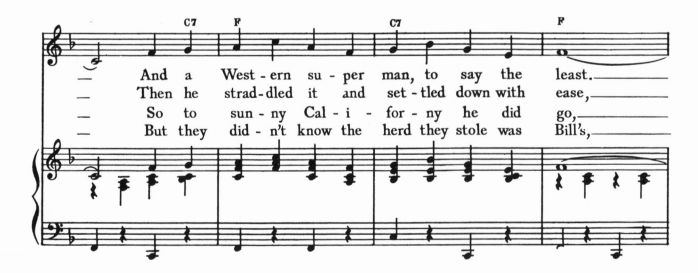

He was the rough-est, tough-est crit-ter, nev-er known to be a
And while that cy-clone bucked and flit-ted Pe-cos rolled a smoke and
And though the gag is kind-a corn-y he brought rain from Cal-i-
And when he caught them crook-ed vill-'ins Pe-cos knocked out all their

quit-ter, 'Cuz he nev-er had no fear of man or beast.____
lit it, And he tamed that orn-'ry wind down to a breeze.____
for-ny, That's the way we got the Gulf of Mex-i-co.____
fill-in's, That's the rea-son why there's gold in them thar hills.____

Refrain

So yip-pee-I ay I-ay____ Yip-pee-I-oh _____ Fer the

tough-est crit-ter West of the A-la-mo.____ 2.Once he
3.Once there
4.Once a

mo._____

Extra Verses

Pecos lost his way while travlin' on the desert
It was ninety miles across the burnin' sand,
He knew he'd never reach the border
If he didn't get some water
So he got a stick and dug the Rio Grande.

So yip-pee-I-ay I-ay Yip-pee-I-oh
Fer the toughest critter West of the Alamo.

6th Verse

Now one day Pecos found his fav'rite dogie missin'
The dogie that was nearest to his heart,
So then he lassoed all the cattle
Clear from Texas to Seattle
That's the way the Texas round-up got its start.

So yip-pee-I-ay I-ay Yip-pee-I-oh
Fer the toughest critter West of the Alamo.

7th Verse

While a tribe of painted Injuns did a war dance
Pecos started shootin' up their little game,
He gave them redskins such a shakeup
That they jumped out from their makeup
That's the way the painted desert got its name.

So yip-pee-I-ay I-ay Yip-pee-I-oh
Fer the toughest critter West of the Alamo.

8th Verse

While reclinin' on a cloud high over Texas
With his gun he made the stars evaporate
Then Pecos saw the stars declinin'
So he left one brightly shinin'
As the emblem of the Lone Star Texas State.

So yip-pee-I-ay I-ay Yip-pee-I-oh
Fer the toughest critter West of the Alamo.

56 Riders In The Sky
1949

Stan Jones (Courtesy of Olive Jones)

When Stan Jones and an old cowpoke named Cap Watts went riding out one day on the D Hill range in southern Arizona, there was unrest in the air. They began to tie down the blades on a windmill when masses of dark, fast-moving clouds appeared on the horizon forming spectral figures. Cap Watts warned prophetically, "Ghost riders!"

Ghost riders are bad omens in the cattle country. They generally appear when fast-moving cold air from one direction collides with warm air from a different direction, a condition that sometimes generates a series of tornadoes. Ominous cloud silhouettes, grouping, regrouping, and backlighted with yellow and sun-red accents, look to the imaginative mind like nothing more than a line of riders racing through the ragged skies. On this day, while helping to secure the windmill from possible wind damage, the youthful Jones heard for the first time the ghostly account of phantom riders in the sky trying to catch the devil's herd. He never forgot the story, and it became the theme for one of the most haunting cowboy songs of all times.

Levi "Cap" Watts worked at times for the D Hill Ranch near Douglas, Arizona. The Texas-born cowboy operated his own "saddle blanket" outfit in the Perilla Mountains east of Douglas for awhile. He never owned much country, but he did have some good Texas steel dust horses, a choice strain for working cattle. In 1910 he sold one to the governor of Sonora, Mexico. Somewhat of a recluse in later years, Cap lived in a dugout in the northeast part of the D Hill Ranch and sat outside in one place on the ground so long that in time his hindquarters wore out their own dugout. The grizzled cowboy died in 1934.

Stanley Davis Jones was born on 5 June 1914 in Douglas, Arizona. He served his country in the U.S. Navy during World War II and earned a degree in zoology at the University of California.

While working as a park ranger in Death Valley in 1949, Jones acted as a guide for movie location scouts during the filming of *Three Godfathers*, starring John Wayne, Harry Carey, Jr., and Pedro Armendariz. He had learned the fundamentals of guitar playing from Arizona cowboys, so it was only natural that he treat the Hollywood group to his own special brand of campfire music. With some reluctance he sang the haunting words to a song he had made up himself from the legend told by Cap Watts many years before. "Riders In The Sky" changed the life of Stan Jones almost overnight. Later in the year he appeared in the Gene Autry movie *Riders in the Sky*, which featured his song. He also wrote the theme song and had a role in the 1951 movie *Whirlwind*, starring Gene Autry. Songs for the John Ford 1950 production *Wagonmaster*, starring Ben Johnson, were written by Stan Jones, and he composed the title song to the John Wayne movie *The Searchers* in 1956. He also wrote compositions for Walt Disney TV and movie films.

The writer, actor, dreamer, and creator of songs died on 13 December 1963 and was buried in his hometown of Douglas, Arizona. As part of the services, Dr. Henry J. Lange, a longtime friend from California, read the words to the song "Resurrectus," written by the deceased in 1950: "Out of the shadows high on a hill, here at last I'm home. And the earth is sweet beneath my feet, for all I see I own. To me belongs the starlight and the leaf on a whispering stream. I own from here to way out there. There's no worry now it seems, I'll see Him in the sunrise or just as day is done—No more to walk in darkness for I know now my cares are none."*

*"Last Respects Are Paid to Stan Jones," (Douglas, Ariz.) *Daily Dispatch*, 18 December 1963.

Riders In The Sky
(A Cowboy Legend)

By
STAN JONES

might - y herd of red - eyed cows he saw A plough - in' thru the
through him as they thun - dered thru the sky For he saw the ri - ders
ev - er on that range up in the sky On hors - es snort - in'
ways to - day or with us you will ride A - try'n to catch the

rag - ged skies _____ And up a cloud - y draw. _____
com - in' hard _____ And he heard their mourn - ful cry. _____
fire _____ As they ride on, hear their cry. _____
dev - il's herd _____ A - cross these end - less skies." _____

Yi - pi - yi - ay, _____

Yi - pi - yi - o, _____ 1. The ghost herd
2. ghost rid - ers
3. ghost rid - ers
4. The

57 Happy Trails 1950

Leonard Franklin Slye was born on 5 November 1911 in Cincinnati, Ohio. Shortly after, his father moved the family on to an Ohio River houseboat to get away from the bustle of city life. The elder Slye purchased a small farm in the Duck Run community near Portsmouth, Ohio, when his son Leonard was eight years old.

In 1930 the Slye family headed for California in a seven-year-old Dodge. After their arrival, Leonard and his brother Stanley played and sang at square dances in the Los Angeles area as the Slye Brothers, but they were not successful at earning money. Leonard then played without pay with Uncle Tom Murray's Hollywood Hillbillies. Later he entered an amateur radio contest in Inglewood as a soloist. He did not win, but the Rocky Mountaineers heard him and the next day asked him to join the group.

In time, he was joined by Bob Nolan and Tim Spencer, who were to figure prominently in his career. When the group disbanded Slye joined another band called the International Cowboys, still singing and playing free of charge. They soon changed their name to the O Bar O Cowboys and toured Arizona, New Mexico, and the Texas Panhandle, making only enough money to pay their way. Following their breakup Slye joined the Texas Outlaws, but he never lost his vision of forming a singing group with Nolan and Spencer. The two finally agreed to join him, and in 1933 the Pioneers Trio, nucleus of the original Sons of the Pioneers, was formed.

Leonard Slye landed some bit parts in motion pictures under the name Dick Weston and in 1937 signed a contract as a singing cowboy with Republic Pictures. Studio executives got together to pick a new name for their future star. The success of cowboy humorist Will Rogers had proved the name to be ideally western in character and sound, so they decided on Rogers. They also wanted a short, alliterative first name. One executive suggested the name Roy meant "king," and that did it. Roy Rogers, "King of the Cowboys," was created.

Frances Octavia Smith was born on 31 October 1912 at the home of her grandparents in Uvalde, Texas. When she was seven years old, the family moved to Osceola, Arkansas. Frances took piano lessons at an early age, but her instructor quit because his student preferred improvising to practicing scales. She continued playing and singing by ear.

After four years in nearby Memphis, Tennessee, Frances moved to Chicago, but there she found only secretarial work. Radio station WHAS in Louisville, Kentucky, gave her a job in 1936 as a female vocalist on the staff and gave her the professional name Dale Evans because it was simple to spell, pronounce, and remember.

Dale tried Chicago again in the late 1930s and became successful as a popular singer with a top Chicago band. She headlined in night clubs as a torch singer and appeared regularly on a CBS radio variety show. A movie agent heard Dale on the radio and called her to Hollywood in 1940 for a

Roy Rogers and Dale Evans

movie career. Four years later she appeared in *The Cowboy and the Senorita* with Roy Rogers and became his regular female lead for future films.

On the evening of 31 December 1947, the "King of the Cowboys" and the "Queen of the West" were married at the Flying L Ranch near Davis, Oklahoma.

It was customary for Roy Rogers to use the expression "happy trails" as a parting wish to someone and as a kindly message above his autograph. One day in 1950, Dale Evans kept humming the phrase over and over and ended up writing in one afternoon the song most associated with them.

The memorable "Happy Trails" was copyrighted in 1951. It became the theme song for "The Roy Rogers Show" on television from 1951 to 1957 and again for "The Roy Rogers and Dale Evans Show" television series from 1962 to 1963. A joint effort by the couple produced a religious version of the song in 1978.

The standard "Happy Trails" was republished in 1981 with its first change, the addition of a verse.

HAPPY TRAILS

Words and Music by
DALE EVANS

Slowly and Tenderly

58 Gunsmoke 1952

The beautiful strains of the theme from the radio and television series "Gunsmoke" are familiar to millions of listeners around the world. Seldom heard, however, are the words to the song. The music was written by Rex Koury as thematic material, but Hollywood music publisher Max Herman saw its possibilities as a song. His friend Glenn Spencer, a member of the famous songwriting team for the Sons of the Pioneers, supplied words for the theme.

Originally published under the title "'Old Trail,'" the song was written for the CBS radio show "Gunsmoke," which aired for the first time in the spring of 1952 with William Conrad as the radio voice of the fictional Dodge City lawman Matt Dillon.

When the popular radio show moved to television in 1955, the title of the theme song was changed to "Gunsmoke," lines were altered or rearranged, and eighth notes were inserted to accommodate the added syllable required when the words "old trail" were replaced by "gunsmoke trail." James Arness assumed the TV role of the resolute Marshal Matt Dillon for its twenty-year-run on CBS from 1955 to 1975.

Rex Koury was organist and musical director for ABC on the West Coast from 1947 to 1958. Early in 1952 he was asked by CBS to compose and supervise the music for the new radio series "Gunsmoke." This is his story of writing the music under unusual circumstances:

I promptly accepted the engagement for the Gunsmoke program. My procedure in writing for a show was to compose all the "interior" music first—the bridges, background music, etc. When that was finished, I tackled the theme, knowing what to assimilate into it. Furthermore, the theme is the most difficult,

Glenn Spencer (Courtesy of Wanda Spencer)

Center, Rex Koury, music composer for the "Gunsmoke" radio and television series, holding the *Downbeat Magazine* Award for the best scoring of a TV series in 1954. *Left*, Willian Conrad, radio's Matt Dillon; *right*, director Bill McDonald. (Courtesy of Rex Koury)

simply because it must appeal to the sponsor, producer, and a myriad of others connected with the show. It is the one piece of music with which a show is instantly identified.

I had been composing all day, doing the interior music, but still the theme remained. I went to bed tired, but knowing that the copy department must have the theme by 10:00 A.M. the following day. At 8:30 A.M., I awoke, dressed, and had breakfast. The deadline was racing ominously upon me! I took a pencil, a magazine, and some manuscript paper into the bathroom, and while sitting there, composed the Gunsmoke theme in ten minutes.*

Reginald St. George Koury was born on 18 March 1912 in London, England. His father had been in the Anglo-Egyptian Sudan with the British government service up until the year before, when the family went back to England. They moved to America in 1913 and settled in New Jersey.

When Rex finished grammar school, his class attended a showing of the motion picture *Abraham Lincoln* as part of a school event. Rex heard a pipe organ for the first time and was captivated by it. He made up his mind to be a theater organist. At

age sixteen he got his first job in the Mayfair Theater in Hillside, New Jersey.

After providing musical background for silent movies, Rex became a solo organist with the RKO circuit and studied with Jesse Crawford. He moved to California in 1934 and played with a dance band. Following World War II, he joined the new ABC in 1947 as an organist, and in 1952 he became the network's musical director for the entire West Coast. It was during the same year that Rex wrote the "Gunsmoke" theme, cues, and underscores for CBS.

Glenn Joseph Spencer, who wrote the words for the song "Gunsmoke," was born in Joplin, Missouri, on 16 August 1910. He was an early musical director for the Sons of the Pioneers, in which his brother, Tim Spencer, was an original performing member. Glenn Spencer died on 19 December 1970 in Simi Valley, California.

*Lloyd E. Klos, "Spanning Three Eras With Rex Koury," *Theatre Organ* 18, no. 6 (December–January 1976–77): 10.

GUNSMOKE
Theme of "Gunsmoke"

Words by
GLENN SPENCER

Music by
REX KOURY

59 High Noon 1952

Had it not been for a song, one of the great non-musical western motion pictures of all times might have been a box office failure. This was the feeling held by the producer and director after the movie's first run-through in the executive studios.

The motion picture *High Noon* was produced with only background music. After viewing the rough cut, tentatively entitled *The Tin Star*, Russian-born composer Dimitri Tiomkin successfully proposed the idea of a theme song that would tell the plot at the beginning of the picture. He worked up a melody and developed the song with Ned Washington lyrics.

Ned Washington (ASCAP)

In spite of the attempt, the first preview of the film in a theater outside Los Angeles was indeed a failure. Tiomkin came up with another idea. He talked the filmmakers into assigning him rights to the song for publication and recording. Cowboy singer Tex Ritter refused an offer to do the song at first but later reconsidered and sang it off-camera for the movie soundtrack.

Despite his classical music training, Dimitri Tiomkin was an unabashed fan of country-western music, and in his disjointed English he instructed Tex Ritter on how to sing the song: "Taxes, you must sing it like this: 'Do not forsake me, oh mine darlink.'"*

Besides having the song introduce the motion picture, fragments of "High Noon" were sung throughout the picture with guitar strumming and thumping to highlight action.

By the time the finished picture was released, a recording of the song by Frankie Laine had become a tremendous success and helped stimulate interest in the movie throughout America. Film critics were almost unanimous in their judgment that much of the success of *High Noon* was due to its musical score. The film become a western classic.

Dimitri Tiomkin was born on 10 May 1899 in St. Petersburg, Russia. He fled his homeland after the 1917 revolution and performed as a concert pianist in Europe. In 1925 Tiomkin made his first visit

*Burt Folkart, "Dimitri Tiomkin, 85, Prolific Composer for Films, Dies," *Los Angeles Times*, 14 November 1979.

Shoot-out scene in *High Noon*. (Saturday Matinee)

Dimitri Tiomkin (Courtesy of the Academy of Motion Picture Arts and Sciences)

to the United States, where he met and married Albertina Rasch, the famous dancer and choreographer. She was called to Hollywood in 1930 to help produce screen musicals for MGM. While there with her Tiomkin created the musical setting for three motion pictures. He eventually composed musical scores for 160 motion pictures and was nominated for an Academy Award twenty-four times, winning four. Two of his Oscars were for *High Noon*, one for the best score and another for the best theme song.

Other western films for which Tiomkin wrote the music were *Duel in the Sun, Gunfight at the O.K. Corral, The Alamo*, and *Giant*. He died in London on 11 November 1979.

Ned Washington won one of his three Academy Awards for the compelling words to "High Noon." Edward M. "Ned" Washington, born in Scranton, Pennsylvania, on 15 August 1901, became one of Hollywood's most prolific lyricists. His western songs include "The Marshal of Wichita," "The Man from Laramie," "Gunfight at the O.K. Corral," "The 3:10 to Yuma," "Broken Arrow," and the TV title song "Rawhide." He died at his home in Beverly Hills, California, on 20 December 1976.

Sung in the Stanley Kramer Production "HIGH NOON"

HIGH NOON
(DO NOT FORSAKE ME)

Lyric by
NED WASHINGTON

Music by
DIMITRI TIOMKIN

294   **High Noon**

60 El Paso 1957

Martin David Robinson and his twin sister, Mamie Ellen Robinson, were born on 26 September 1925 in a two-room house in the desert north of Glendale, Arizona. Their father was Polish and their mother was of European, Paiute Indian, and Mexican descent. The father left the family in 1937, and young Martin spent much of his time around cowboys and watching Gene Autry movies on Saturdays. He caught wild horses with his brother in the Arizona mountains and broke them to ride and sell. He also rode the rails as a youthful hobo.

Western stories that he read, combined with tales of the Old West by his maternal grandfather, Robert "Texas Bob" Heckle, a former frontier scout and Indian fighter, were an inspiration to him. Both were profoundly influential sources of his music.

Martin Robinson joined the U.S. Navy in 1942, when he was only seventeen years old, and learned to play the guitar while stationed in the Solomon Islands. Following his discharge in 1945, he formed his own musical group, the K Bar Boys, and began regular radio broadcasts over KTYL in Mesa, Arizona. A year later he moved to KPHO Phoenix and assumed the stage name Marty Robbins.

The blossoming star signed a record contract with Columbia in 1951 and became a regular performer in 1952 at the Grand Ole Opry in Nashville, Tennessee.

While driving through El Paso to a family Christmas gathering in Phoenix in 1955, Marty Robbins

Marty Robbins

got the idea for a song. He had always thought of El Paso as the typical western town and the place where the West really began. The following Christmas holiday season, he made the trip for the same reason and again thought of writing a song about El Paso. On his third consecutive trip through El Paso in 1957, the song took shape in his mind. The words started flowing faster than he could have

Robert "Texas Bob" Heckle, Indian fighter and scout for General George Crook and other army officers during the Indian Wars in Wyoming and Montana during the 1870s. Texas Bob was an inspiration to his grandson, Marty Robbins. (Earle Forrest Collection, Museum of Northern Arizona)

written them down even if he had been able to do so. To him it was like watching a great western movie. When he reached Phoenix ten hours later Marty wrote down the words. He had little trouble remembering them because the scenes from the song were like scenes from the movie he had envisioned.

Although it was unknown to Marty at the time, Rosa's Cantina, his fictitious setting for the song, had actually existed around the turn of the century and was the most popular border joint in El Paso at that time. The bar, or at least a part of it, still stands and does business under the same name.

Marty tried to record "El Paso" in New York in 1958, but recording executives believed the song—at four-and-a-half minutes—too long for normal radio playing time. It was not until a year later that he recorded it in Nashville as the lead song in his LP album *Gunfighter Ballads and Trail Songs*. The record helped bridge the gap between country and pop music by becoming number 1 on both popu-

larity charts in 1959 and selling more than one million copies. Two years later Marty became the first country and western singer ever to win the coveted Grammy Award. Somehow he found time to write a short western novel, *The Small Man*, published in 1966.

In 1966 Marty Robbins also wrote the eight-minute-long "Felenna (From El Paso)," a sequel to his sensational ballad-type song about the West Texas city. He followed with another in 1976 called "El Paso City" and had plans to continue the saga with two more related songs, "The Mystery of El Paso" and "Adios Amigo El Paso."*

Marty Robbins survived three devastating high speed crashes in race car competition, two heart attacks, and a triple-bypass heart operation. On 11 October 1982, he was inducted into the Country Music Hall of Fame. In less than two months he underwent quadruple-bypass surgery and died of cardiac arrest six days later, on 8 December 1982. Millions of people mourned the death of Marty Robbins. Even the normally clear, dry skies of El Paso shed tears the day after he died.†

Although adept at singing country, gospel, Hawaiian, Mexican, pop, and rockabilly songs, Marty Robbins accented the cowboy and western style of songwriting and performing in the fashion of his idol Gene Autry.

*Ronnie Pugh, "Notes on the Music," *Country & Western Classics: Marty Robbins*, Time-Life Records, Alexandria, Va., 1983.

†Charles Edgren, "Mourners Missing from Rosa's Cantina," *El Paso* (Texas) *Herald-Post*, 10 December 1983.

El Paso

By
MARTY ROBBINS

Moderato

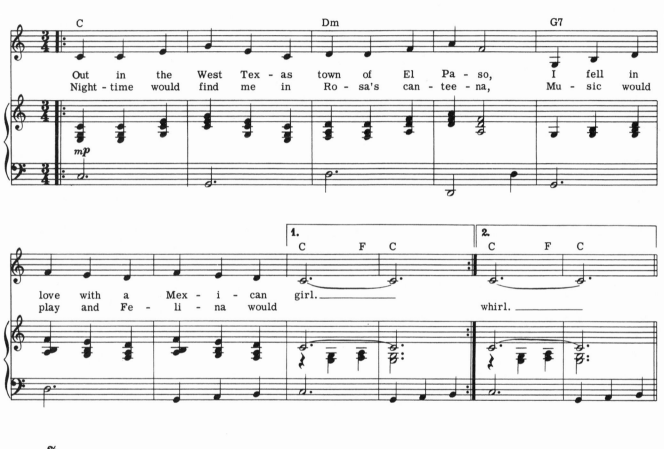

Out in the West Tex - as town of El Pa - so, I fell in
Night - time would find me in Ro - sa's can - tee - na, Mu - sic would

love with a Mex - i - can girl.
play and Fe - li - na would whirl.

1. C F C
2. C F C

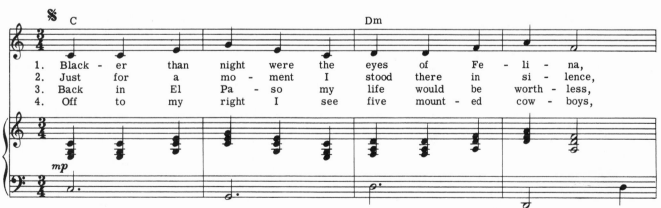

1. Black - er than night were the eyes of Fe - li - na,
2. Just for a mo - ment I stood there in si - lence,
3. Back in El Pa - so my life would be worth - less,
4. Off to my right I see five mount - ed cow - boys,

West Tex - as wind. _____
hors - es were tied. _____
lone in the dark. _____
pain in my side. _____

Dash - ing and dar - ing, a drink he was shar - ing with wick - ed Fe -
I caught a good one, it looked like it could run, _____ Up on its
May - be to - mor - row a bul - let will find me, To - night noth - ing's
Though I am try - ing to stay in the sad - dle, _____ I'm get - ting

li - na, the girl that I loved. _____ So in an - ger I
back and a - way I did ride. _____ Just as fast as I
worse than this pain in my heart. _____ And at last here I
wear - y un - a - ble to ride. _____ But my love for Fe -

chal - lenged his right for the love of this maid - en, Down went his
could from the West Tex - as town of El Pa - so, Out to the
am on the hill o - ver - look - ing El Pa - so, I can see
li - na is strong and I rise where I've fal - len, Though I am

INDEX